THE FIERCEST FIGHT

A documented account of the struggle against Apartheid in South Africa

by
EARL DENMAN

Foreword
by
Gonville ffrench-Beytagh
formerly Dean of Johannesburg

CHURCHMAN PUBLISHING
1985

THE FIERCEST FIGHT
was first published in 1985 by

CHURCHMAN PUBLISHING LIMITED
117 Broomfield Avenue
Worthing
West Sussex
BN14 7SF

ISBN 1 85093 0120

Distributed to the book trade by

BAILEY BROS. & SWINFEN LIMITED
Warner House
Folkestone
Kent
CT19 6PH

Churchman's agents in Canada
Jonathan Gould Books of Winnipeg

Printed in Great Britain by Whitstable Litho Limited

Contents

Personal involvement in the major issues of our times grows unavoidable, and this may be to our advantage, because we need to care for others, thereby relieving ourselves of stifling selfishness. One inhibiting factor is that we cannot be experts on every topic that comes to our notice, nor even the few which are of particular interest to us. We need information: before we can advance we require authority and guidance.

One of the main considerations of today is the South African crisis, which simply will not go away of its own accord. With the facts at my command I have assembled them here for the benefit of the uninitiated, the would-be standard bearers who were not on the spot when apartheid came into being but wish to know where they stand in relation to it. The text is set out in such a way as to represent a kaleidoscope of events, and I have endeavoured to make it as easily readable and assimilative as possible. My own experiences are recounted only to highlight my authority by indicating 'I was there.'

No matter what our station in life, we acquire a set of values. This being so, I invite readers to page through this work in order to assess its contents and then, if so inclined, proceed beyond mere perusal, entering into the very heart of the matter. Apartheid is, to the intellect, as grave in its consequences as the nuclear armament race which threatens us with physical extinction.

Here is a challenge to the thoughts and aspirations of the individual. Pay no heed to race or colour. They are but incidental. Do not permit extraneous matters to intrude. Disregard all other contentious issues in order to see this one in its proper context. This is not Brixton or Guatemala or El Salvador or the Middle East. Our commitment must be limited: we are not dealing with North American Indians or Australian aboriginals, nor with Maori land rights. Do not be sidetracked by diversionary tactics, 'Oh yes, but what about . . .' In this special case the struggle is for the political and social rights of a majority of citizens in the land of their origin.

Lose your identity awhile, the better to take on the problems of others. Know what it means to suffer deprivation, to the extent of losing homeland, home and true identity. Share imprisonment and torture with the damned. Undergo privation in cells of solitude. Enter wholly, unreservedly, and emerge with your own set of values.

I am aware of the pitfalls confronting a work of serious nature which makes no pretence at light entertainment. Also I know that unanimity of thought is beyond attainment, though if anything invites it, apartheid does. There are two powerful considerations when striving towards unilateral purpose and involvement *now*, before time runs out. They are as follows:

1. Increasingly there is criticism of the German public for its failure to oppose Hitler and so avert World War II. Criticism is all very well, if we ourselves are free from blame. But are we? Here is a chance to prove ourselves. A similarly brutal regime exists. Are we to oppose it, or slide into default? If the latter, then we have no right to condemn the Germans for their vacillations under Hitler.

2. It can be conjecture only, but this question has been put by an African: Would the Good Samaritan have intervened if he had chanced upon the scene earlier, while the victim was being beaten and robbed? We cannot know. But *this* we can know. In our time, indigenous Africans have been beaten and now are being robbed. Shall we disregard the danger to ourselves and go to their aid? Or wait until they have been robbed and left? What is it to be, Discretion or Heroism? Delaying until the danger has passed, we may be accounted Good, but what of it, if our Courage is in question?

In the event of continuing vacillation, who will be to blame? Primarily America, secondly Britain. They provide the props supportive of apartheid and have only to remove them. But they will take no steps to this end unless pressured, and this is where we come in, the ordinary citizens. Independently there is little we can do, but collectively we can ensure that history does not declare us lacking in moral fibre or the intent to be in time to avert the worst of consequences.

The soil of our country
    is destined to be the scene
    of THE FIERCEST FIGHT
    and the sharpest battles
    to rid our continent
    of the last vestiges
    of white minority rule.
                    Nelson Mandela

Foreword

by
Canon Gonville ffrench-Beytagh
*formerly – until his banishment from South Africa –
Dean of Johannesburg*

It is not really possible for a white man to get under the skin of a black man and to feel in his bones the history of several hundred years of deprivation, indignity, persecution and brutality which the black man in South Africa has experienced. Mr Denman has, I think, come as near to it as possible.

In this book he brings that history up-to-date. He sets out the contemporary facts as they have been recorded in the courts and in the news media in South Africa. I, myself, can vouch for the truth of what he records. He comments on these facts in a series of poems, with a passion that is deeply felt. They stirred up my anger once again at the intolerable injustice of the situation in that country. I hope that they will stir yours also. He then comments on these matters in a series of reflections which I commend to you. I particularly commend his introductory summary of the origins and anatomy of that misshapen monster which we call Apartheid.

I hope and believe that this book will do a great deal to strengthen the active opposition to Apartheid which needs to be fought on every possible front. It is a book which stands in the tradition of *Naught For Your Comfort* and *Cry The Beloved Country*. I am grateful to be asked to write this Foreword and to be associated with the publishing house responsible for bringing out such a superb and noble book.

Gonville ffrench-Beytagh

In South Africa a situation has developed akin to that in which Arjuna, at the battle of Kurukshetra, is overcome with sorrow at the thought of the fury about to be unleashed. As told in the Bhagavad-Gita, he is averse to the killing of his kinsmen and wonders on which side to take his stand. So it is for us also. There is the same inevitability. It is too late to turn back from warring. Shortly after Sharpeville there was the chance to avert the ultimate catastrophe but it was not accepted, and it is no use repining at this late hour. Like Arjuna, we see that our own kith and kin are involved. It should not matter. Considerations of race and colour only serve to cloud the issue. They should not sway us. A principle is at stake; this is the overriding factor.

It is a case of which side to take, with no possibility of neutrality. It is a straight fight with no alternative, no intermediate choice. Indeed, to seek an alternative is to turn aside from reality, and to do that, where principle is at stake, negates the principle. Once our moral conviction is established we must remain steadfast, undeviating.

There can be no compromise, because compromise is not a principle in itself, but a deflection from principle. It is an escape mechanism, cowardly rather than courageous.

That there should be people of conflicting thought should not surprise or discourage us. As we gain allies, so we shall make enemies. We should not hate those who contest our views. In any fight there must be opponents, and in victory we should be magnanimous. Here again it is a matter of principle, and before the fight is over we should prepare ourselves for magnanimity. Victory is our aim, not vengeance.

Expedience is not our line. We are the forward thinkers, the motivators moving in the right direction. Herein lies our basic strength. Our obligation is to act, not react; to act timeously, not react when all is too late. There is no virtue in pragmatism. It is but an excuse for dalliance.

This will explain our absolute, inflexible determination to eradicate the evil in our midst. Nevertheless, we must provide an avenue of escape for those who oppose us, and this should be found in our resolve not to sink to vindictiveness once victory has been gained.

Where to stand in the coming armed conflict, the fiercest fight? My story should help readers to make up their minds. For me, with my roots in wildness, the way was made open. Being a man of nature, racism did not blur my vision. Nor was I swayed by considerations of ease or of monetary gain. Also I was helped in large measure through my early contacts with Africans on a mutual basis of give and take. For most others there is bound to be hesitation and doubt. My story, in all its simplicity, may help to relieve doubt and point the way to decisiveness.

Before long the entire world will become involved on one side or the other. For apartheid is of worldwide concern. Likewise a day will arise when our struggle will repose in the past. It will become a part of history, and it is this that matters more than any historian's assessment of it. We cannot hope to change history to any great extent, and it is not to this vain end that we pit our resources. No, our vision is not of a better world, but of a fairer one, and this lies within our scope.

Foreword

Part 1 . . . The Historian Speaks

If outside pressures had been effective
our own non-violence would have been enough
Govan Mbeki

My manuscript traces the South African conflict through all its phases, starting with Banishment and moving on to Martyrdom, Exile, Incitement, Detention (90-Day/180-Day), Agitation, Sabotage, and not excluding those inseparables from any human encounter, the Intimidators and Informers. It does this by means of:

1   News reports, mostly harking back to the 1960s, which provide a background of irrefutable facts.
2   An interlacing of verse.
3   My own reflections, based upon experience.

The news reports lend authenticity and provide a historic basis, placing into perspective the fateful 1950s, the catastrophic 1960s, eras of unrelieved oppression and suffering for the opponents of apartheid. They point to the inevitably of armed conflict, despite the odds involved, which are all but insuperable.

All too many apartheid supporters are inclined to see the South African situation as a recent development, whereas it has been long, long in building up. At this late stage no one can say where or when the spirit of revolt first stirred to life. The best we can do, reliably, is take as our starting point the uprisings in Sekhukuniland, Witzieshoek, Zeerust, Marico, Pondoland. From these tribal regions the hard core of resistance moved to the urban ghettos, there to gather force. During the years of Malan, Strijdom, Verwoerd, there was talk of revolution. Under Vorster and Botha feelings hardened and thoughts turned to war. Only the means were lacking.

Indeed, how do the deprived masses, unarmed, prepare for battle? As my manuscript shows, they find their way through suffering and sorrow. Loss upon loss until at length there is nothing left to lose. After defeat in a succession of pitched battles, with assegais opposed to guns, the black tribes were kept subservient by means of deep and lasting humiliation. Having lost their freedom to roam at will within the land of their birth, they lost their valour, their pride, their all – except the unfathomable spirit of belonging, the inner sense of attachment to mother earth. There is nothing more basic than this. The feeling constitutes the most heartfelt prayer of all.

Rising from defeat, slowly, laboriously, they came to recognise themselves as true heirs of the African soil. There followed the lessons of Algeria, Kenya, Guinea-Bissau, Mozambique, Angola, and not the least, Viet Nam: the human spirit, rooted in home soil, backed by numerical sufficiency, is unconquerable.

To me as a writer the driving force is to expose apartheid as fully as possible, without equivocation. In one respect I have an advantage over most other writers; I have seen the situation in its making. For good or ill, it was my lot to arrive in South Africa while Smuts was in office, and live under four successive National Party prime ministers, Malan, Strijdom, Verwoerd, Vorster. They were the real architects of apartheid South Africa, especially Dr H. F. Verwoerd. He, more than anyone else, dictated the course of events for years to follow and made inevitable the violence leading to armed struggle.

Having the facts at my command, I have assembled them here. Taking everything into consideration – the long build-up with its associated humiliations, aspects of race and colour, the religious, philosophic and political implications, widespread international repercussions, and particularly the fact that South Africa is mineral rich and represents the last bastion of Western colonialism – it is likely to be The Fiercest Fight.

I do not think that war will be declared at any stage. The struggle will just go grinding on the way it has been doing for years, intensifying, the accompanying bitterness and divisiveness increasing, the associated hate proliferating. Renewed efforts will be made to enlist American military support for Afrikanerdom, using the communist bogey as a pretext. I hope these efforts will prove unavailing, leaving the issue a clear one between good and evil as pertaining to the South African situation. There has been more than enough hypocrisy and double dealing already. However, Americans are so politically naive, so blinded by anti-labour, anti-socialism and anti-communism that they are likely to fall into the trap.

Meanwhile there is an increasing drive to deprive the non-white majority of a common identity. Under the most degrading terms of apartheid they are to be Xhosas, Zulus, Vendas, Fingos, Coloureds, Indians, but not South Africans. So, the sooner the name South Africa is expunged and a new one bestowed, the better. Azania is the most likely choice, with all residents identified as Azanians. Anything rather than the unimaginative name under which so many have suffered for so long.

While events take their tragic course, let us take stock of the current devices for the perpetuation of apartheid. These may be listed as follows:

1   The propaganda that apartheid legislation is being relaxed and that all will come right of its own accord. Only give it time and *Alles sal reg kom*.
2   The Bantustan concept, with the stripping of South African citizenship from all non-whites. Nowadays, 'Resettlement' goes hand-in-hand with the Bantustans. Like apartheid itself, it is a deceit, a whitewashing term.
3   The swamping of non-white aspirations through recruitment drives for white immigrants, preferrably from Holland, West Germany, England, in that order.
4   For selfish purpose, to serve as a barrier against clamour for radical change, the establishment of a secure, contented work force forming a middle class of non-whites.
5   Splitting of the main opposition, with 'homeland' leaders set against ANC and PAC leaders in exile.
6   The suggestion that sporting contacts are breaking down barriers. (Regardless of the fact that this is no game that is being played. With so many lives at stake, of adults and young, male and female, it is irrational to believe that entertainment, or in other terms sport, might influence the outcome)

With regard to the first point, of course apartheid is being relaxed in small measure, but in other, bigger ways it is being built up. As petty pinpricks are relieved, so the Bantustans, coupled with 'Resettlement', are coming into effect, and they represent the ultimate in apartheid. Hence the governmental need for TIME. In any case, the tempo could not have been sustained. All events peak, then recede. With apartheid the peak was reached in the 1960s, before many of its present supporters were born.

As my backgroundings of news reports indicate, subsequent events have been seasoned by that intensely provocative period during which so very many opponents of apartheid were banned, banished, exiled, imprisoned, put to death, placed under house arrest or otherwise silenced. We should not allow ourselves to be deceived by propaganda nor cajoled into letting bygones be bygones for the sake of placating a few. The inclination to do so is understandable, but it bodes ill for the future when we permit the past to be forgotten. We cannot carry with us the burden of the ages. No, but we are responsible for the direction of affairs during our lifetime, and this involvement ensures our association with the past, our indebtedness to the future. To forgive and forget is the easy way out. It lacks depth, loyalty, courage. History records too much brutality, too much deprivation for it to be written off as if it were no more than a bad debt. Too many lives have been blighted, too much potential talent has been wasted, too many homes and marriages have been wrecked. Forgiveness is all very well, but not when it invokes betrayal. No matter how tolerant we may consider ourselves as individuals, the collective memory is not so short that the dead, the banned, the banished, the exiles, the imprisoned, the tortured can be cast out of mind so readily. Martyrdom alone ensures that sacrifice on such a large scale shall not be in vain. Already there are martyrs enough in the fight against apartheid. My apologies for harping on the past so much, but would it be fair, let alone just, to forgive and forget the monstrous wrongs done to the peasants who started the revolt, and to such as Chief Luthuli, Robert Sobukwe, Nelson Mandela, Mapetla Mohapi, Steven Biko, Walter Sisulu, Oliver Tambo and countless others? To erase the past in order to make a fresh start from unsound premises, is this the best we can hope to accomplish?

Do not be deceived by pretentious aims and ill-conceived words. The leopard apartheid does not change its spots. All that is taking place is political slight-of-hand. Let me put it this way:

Certainly there is relaxation of
apartheid in sport. Athletes are
allowed to take part in
non-segregated sporting events
. . . . while those not adept in fields
of sport are dispossessed,
'resettled' in impoverished
'homelands'.

Agreed that the wealthier
non-whites are permitted to
enter hotels and bars hitherto
out of bounds to them . . . . while an increasing number of
poor unwanteds are bundled
off to 'resettlement' in
so-called 'homelands'.

Admittedly, upper echelons of
the non-white work force,
especially Coloureds, are now
enabled to climb the rungs of
industry and commerce . . . . . while the disadvantaged are
hounded and sent packing,
'Resettled'.

Separate entrances and exits
have been abolished in places . while tens of thousands,
unable to avail themselves of
the facilities, have been
'returned' by train or bus to
homelands which some have
not seen before. That is, they
have been Resettled.

Parks have been opened to
mixed races . . . . only to be closed again, to the
extent of being fenced.

Beach apartheid on certain
inferior beaches is relaxed here
. . . . only to be reintroduced there.

Set out in this manner, it will be understood what is meant by
slight-of-hand, giving with one hand, taking with the other,
relaxing the grip here, intensifying it there, endeavouring by

any means to retain the out-of-balance in favour of white racism. If the dispossessed do not tumble to the grim prospect very soon they will be stripped of all they once owned.

Equally clearly exposed by the foregoing with its double faceted layout is the fact that there can be no neutral stance in relation to apartheid. One must be for it or against it. My aim is to set out the facts bluntly, with no holds barred. Readers should be under no delusion as to what lies ahead as a consquence of all that has happened.

Here I must rely upon poetry, for it would be difficult indeed to bare my thoughts in any other way.

THE HOLOCAUST

The setting, tinder dry, invites the spark.
Too late now to dampen rising discontent.
The time for change was long, long ago,
    before the grave was dug and hope interred,
    before the mound of hate, of chance deferred,
    before the headstone was inscribed, R.I.P.
Too late for loving care, for sympathy,
    too late your tears of remorse,
    now the only recourse
    the quintessential pyre.

Fire, fire, ravage and raze, frenzied fire
    scourge and cleanse, sacrificial purifier,
    flame, flame, billow and blaze,
    the sole agency to erase
    the contaminated past.

Fire can provide warmth, fire can be a friend.
Fire can incinerate, fire can be a fiend.

The flames, reaching up,
    mingle with the fire-god's wrath,
    mushrooming, they envelop the god's troth.
Man's rampage against nature turns
    into nature's rampage against man. It burns
    with white-hot fury, a conflagration
    at the heart of which lies purification.

Fire, fire, ravage and raze, frienzied fire
    scourge and cleanse, sacrificial purifier,
    flame, flame, billow and blaze,
    the sole agency to erase
    the irretrievable past.

Foreword

Part 2 . . . The Poet Speaks

Much reliance is placed upon poetry in my endeavour to seek clarity. Why? Because it probes to the heart of matters more surely than any other form of writing. Like music, it is basic to humanity. Stirring music excites response. So does poetry. Especially where it relies upon symbolism, poetry plumbs the depths of human emotion, provides our nearest approach to an otherwise elusive truth. What better could there be than poetry as a means of unravelling the knots of confusion, of exposing the deceits, the dishonesties of unjust racist laws? Whereas apartheid stands for apartness, poetry stands for togetherness. Its entire structure rests with harmony, likening one object to another, bringing together separate notes, as with music. It brings together, it does not seek fragmentation. Where there are natural differences, it suggests similarities. Consequently, as the very converse to separation, it is a fitting opponent of apartheid, which attempts to divide on the grounds of race and colour in an endeavour to perpetuate white hegemony.

As will be gathered, in my poetry I have not dispensed with rhyme while not being regimented by it. A degree of discipline does no harm. Often, where words are concerned, it helps in probing the elusive truth more surely than does loose verse. Faint rhyme is resorted to at times, and again nothing is lost, while often it yields its own gain.

Surprisingly, this poetry which forms the meat in the sandwich came readily and easily and did not take long, despite the fact that it had to be written spasmodically while coping with a full-time job in industry. The reason is this: in order to compose it I had to set aside all considerations of self and enter wholly into the lives of others. In rapid succession I had to be a refugee, a detainee, an inciter, an agitator, an exile, a saboteur. . . . While being The Other there was no reason for me to tire or age, because I was not being Me.

To slough off the problems of work and settle down to writing, all within minutes, presented no problem. I was inspired to write urgently because of the pressing needs of others, of those whose mantles fell upon me, whose lives of deprivation I entered into. It could have been a shattering experience. Instead, it was all so easy and so inwardly rewarding. I have read somewhere that it does one's soul good to try and do well for other people. So it proved in this instance.

Poetry itself has passed through many phases, and mine I deign to call Purposeful Poetry, in that it is set to use with intent. It is unashamedly utilitarian. In parts it is philosophical, necessarily so. A little more philosophy and less reliance upon drink and drugs, medicines and noise, could be of advantage in this modern world of our fashioning.

My poetry combines the politics of resistance with factual history and actual reportage. Truly, some of it is pure reportage, and none the worse for this, because most of those who bear the touch of martyrdom, such as Mandela, Mbeki, Biko, were gifted with a poetic turn of phrase. Therefore when quoting them I have done little or nothing to change the original wording.

Foreword

Part 3 . . . Personal Reflections

My recountings, especially those in verse, are intended to draw attention to the plight of others, not myself. To this end, it was my heartfelt wish not to be identified by name, race, colour, all of which I consider irrelevant. If anything, I should have preferred to be known as The Quiet Rebel, a descriptive name applied in both Africa and India, strange to relate. However, that has proved impractical.

This being so, nevertheless I ask readers to disregard my identity, dealing with it as many birds deal with food when providing sustenance for their young – absorb, digest, regurgitate. Allow me to slide back into anonymity. (This is not asking too much, for I do it all along with time and age. For it is not clock time and calendar months that matter, but the Seasons, which give time and meaning to all that happens).

Now it will be asked, 'How can a white man speak for Africans, Coloureds, Indians?'

The short answer is 'Easily, if he is a poet'. Philosophers speak for the world. Just so, true poets speak for all humanity, not merely for themselves.

Thus, for a poet to speak for others, regardless of colour, comes naturally.

Places mentioned in text for which
there is insufficient space on map:

Alexandra Township; immediately north of
  Johannesburg on road to Pretoria.
Breakfastvlei; between Grahamstown and
  Kingwilliamstown, about half way.
Cradock; 60km north of Somerset East.
Emmarentia; Johannesburg district.
Kabah Location; Uitenhage.
Kwazakele; Port Elizabeth district.
Hercules; Pretoria suburb.
Linden; Johannesburg suburb.
New Brighton; Port Elizabeth.
Onrusrivier; near Hermanus.
Rivonia (Lilliesleaf Farm); Johannesburg
  suburb.
Walmer; Port Elizabeth.

Bantustans

Transkei . . . . A, B, C on map.
BophuthaTswana . . . . . 1, 2, 3, 4, 5, 6, 7 on
       map.
Ciskei
Venda

Note: BophuthaTswana shows the ridiculous,
desperate nature of the Bantustan
concept. Split into seven sectors widely
scattered, it illustrates the
divide-and-rule policy taken to
extraordinary degree. No towns of real
importance are incorporated, hence the
higgledy-piggledy network. Excluded,
as from official maps, is KwaZulu,
because Chief Gatsha Buthelezi, leader of
the six million Zulus, refuses to accept
homeland independence. It, too, is split
into small scattered pockets.

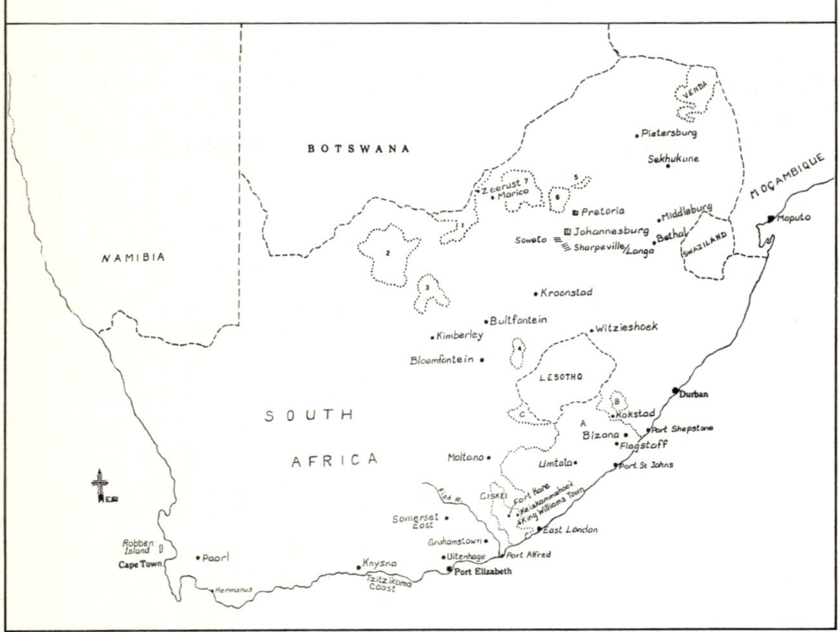

xxii

1

In the Beginning . . .

I was in South Africa the day apartheid arrived.

This may sound preposterous. How could anything as intangible as apartheid arrive so suddenly that it can be said to have arrived on a certain day? Yet that was the way it appeared to me. It came like a thunderclap without a heralding flash of lightning. To others too, it came like a bolt from the blue.

In those days there were no investigative reporters to provide a leakage of information. The backroom boys in Pretoria, in close liaison with Verwoerd, were cock-a-hoop without saying why. Government supporters gloated openly, for no known reason. Opposition forces remained silent, which was not un-usual. Rumours were rife; there was speculation, hushed conversation, but nothing more. For once the bush telegraph failed to notify those normally dependent upon it as a means of communication. Non-whites knew only what they gathered from their masters and mistresses in gleanings of kitchen talk.

Something was in the offing, but what? I have seen cattle with heads raised, sniffing the air, sensing an approaching storm. So it was for most of us; we sensed, but could not know.

Then came the WORD, giving to racism a wider reality and to discrimination a deeper distinction. Like the first word uttered in the universe, it gathered force until it assumed a power of its own, reverberating, penetrating to the farthest corners. But, unlike the original word, heralding knowledge of good and evil, this one presaged unilateral gloom and misery for those destined to bear the brunt of it.

To be specific, I was at Halfway House, midway between Johannesburg and Pretoria, on the day when apartheid arrived. I was editor of the magazine *African Wild Life* at the time, and as a member of the Magazine Committee I attended the quarterly meetings held half way between the commercial capital, Johannesburg, and the administrative centre, Pretoria. It was customary for us to chat awhile afterwards, and on this occasion,

1

with tension acting as a catalyst, we turned to the one topic ordinarily taboo – politics.

Listening intently while adding nothing to the conversation, I gathered that Verwoerd was in the process of sweeping clean after a brief spell of settling into office. He stood revealed as the strong man of Afrikanerdom and its potential saviour. In National Party ranks there was no one to dispute his leadership. The Opposition was in disarray, to such an extent that it served only to sustain Verwoerd and his followers in their righteousness. Without it, there would have arisen cries of "Dictatorship!" Better a milk and sop opposition than none at all.

Suddenly the Word was introduced. It came from the mouth of a stocky Afrikaner, a hard core Nationalist. Holding an important Government post, he was in a position to speak with authority. Before his small, hushed audience, he rolled the new word off his tongue with relish, slowly, gaining for it all the impact he could muster. He gave the word an intonation impossible to express in print. 'Apartheid', he said, but he made it sound like a cross between *apart-hate* and *aparth-hate*. He did not speak the word so much as spit it out. He held an undisguised loathing for 'kaffirs' (never Africans) and in his voice there was something akin to venom. Reflected in his manner and echoed in his tone, he left no doubt as to the new word's harshness, the hate embodied in it. A fervent explanation followed, with paeons of praise for Verwoerd. The word was repeated. There was a stunned silence. To say that we were spellbound may be trite but it is true. The word was like a suckling babe destined to grow into a monster, and by some prescience we were aware of this to the extent of being struck dumb.

This was history in the making, unfolding before us, and the truth took time to seep through. In my confusion, thinking to drown my ignorance, I remained silent. As a deep thinker I am a sluggish one and do not come up with apt responses very readily. Despite this, the word must have struck a chord in my imagination, for I was saddened as well as silenced.

Listening to the man, a deep despondency gripped me, at the same time paving the way to a new resolve. Had I but known, that day was to provide a turning point in my life. For the non-whites it was to bring despair greater than ever, the old agonies intensified, the divisions between them and their masters widened and made more difficult to bridge.

The word spread, firstly to every nook and cranny of South Africa, then to all quarters of the globe. As it travelled, so it snowballed, gaining notoriety and mounting approbrium. Mention South Africa abroad, and apartheid was bound to enter into the conversation. No word has come to symbolise a nation's policy more than this. In years to come I would travel far, but wherever I went the word had reached there before me, even to the remotest places.

Really, apartheid was *baaskap* as before, though not so clearly defined. *Baaskap* was too brutally truthful. Our modern era is one of increasing complexities; technology demands an end to simplicity. Nothing must be seen for what it is in essence. So it can be said that apartheid is *baaskap* brought up to date. During Strijdom's brief powerhouse reign there was the plain, straightforward policy of lording it over others. The blacks were down, the whites stood over them. *Baaskap* was the term in vogue. There was no vaguery about it, no contrivance. It was a word brooking no nonsense. It meant 'white man boss'. It sounded hard and harsh, fittingly.

By contrast, apartheid was meant to be the great deceiver.

The outstanding attribute of the new word was its mesmerising effect. In this it took after its founder, Dr Hendrick Verwoerd, whose brand of politics embodied hypnosis. His face looked out at us daily from our newspapers. He was not the most photographed of men, and usually it was the same photograph showing the cool, calm exterior, reflecting the composure of a man totally competent, worthy of trust, wise, urbane, bland, unsmiling but not grim visaged, a modern Buddha but more serene. In one word, suave.

The impression was of a man utterly dependable, capable of resolving the most complex problems, a man of concrete, not to yield.

Unfortunately for those who seek to subdue the masses, in every society there arises a hard core of opposition which defeats unanimity. Always there are some who turn to embrace a contrary point of view. I, for one, took an instinctive dislike to the father figure as projected. To me, Verwoerd looked so suave as to be sinister. His appearance was so smooth as to suggest a westernised Rasputin, all the more untrustworthy for not sporting a beard, for there was nothing to relieve the hypnotic spell, the bland indifference of his gaze.

Smooth he may have seemed on the surface, like a duck paddling on calm waters, but was it not the masquerade of a politician striving against the tide of history, which runs strongly against tyrants who seek to divert its course to their own advantage? He sought to separate us physically through the creation of Bantustans and mentally by damming every estuary of social intercourse. But to do this he had to ignore the flood of events serving to bring mankind together. Intuitively I distrusted the man and disliked the new word. Before long I came to despise the man and loathe the new word which he had introduced, apartheid.

With astonishing rapidity the word was accepted into every language of significance, without need for quotation marks or italics or interpretation. And not without reason, for it affects all, inside and outside its country of origin. No nation can be free of its implications. Soon, as the coined word acquired significance, so it lost its early enchantment. Before long, in a liberated world lacking swearwords, it was adopted as a ready substitute.

Too late, South Africa's apartheidists learnt their mistake. They had been too eager to follow, as in a trance, their hallowed leader. Apologists moved in to try and salvage the crisis. In a tragi-comedy of errors they wriggled and squirmed in their endeavours to provide the word with new twists if not new meanings. Apartheid was said to be *separate development*. But to outsiders, separation and development constitute a contradiction in terms. How can there be development in isolation? How can the non-whites, centuries behind in technology, hope to catch up while kept apart? (Or are they not supposed to make headway, in which case apartheid is a fraud). To quote one example of many, the ancient Britons did not develop through separation from their invaders, but in association with them. If the Romans had herded the conquered Britons into a patchwork of small states on the west coast of England, calling them Britustans, how could the beaten tribes have advanced to Empire and world commerce? Then how can the non-whites of

South Africa advance except by example and through direct learning?

Parallel development was presented as an alternative to separate development, but it was seen for what it was, a mere trading of words. So apartheid became *discrimination*, but the word proved distasteful in a world of mixed populations, irretrievably on its way to internationalism. Apartheid then gave way to *differentiation*, which lends itself more readily to a tactical play of words, so beloved of diplomats. Dr Anton Rupert, best known of the Afrikaner industrialists and financiers of his day, suggested that apartheid may sound better as *medebestaan*, meaning co-existence. How foolish to think that by a change of words the old offence might disappear, or the national character be softened overnight by a rearrangement of symbols. Dr Koornhof invented *plural democracies*, an arithmetic version of the same standards of double dealing. Dr Treurnicht came up with *plurality of societies*, meaning separate access to equal institutions. *Cultural pluralism* was another juggling with words to offset the harm resulting from apartheid. According to Dr A. L. Geyer, another apartheid apologist, 'Apartheid does not mean *baaskap* over other racial groups.' He failed to state what it does mean.

Words, words, words. We may abhor violence, but we see it daily in its making. Modern generations are sickened by hypocrisy and seek release from it. No crystal ball is required to show that, when the play on words has ended there must be recourse to guns, guns, guns.

Still the word survives. Apartheid. Meaning apartness through hate.

On the contrary, 'Unity is Strength.' The nation's coat of arms proclaims it. 'Unity is Strength.' The motto mocks those who discredit the truth. 'Unity is Strength.' And sudden as a tropic nightfall there was apartheid to disavow the truth.

In spite of all this the word survives, conceived of hatred, born of fear. It has grown too strong to be killed easily. It is one word, more than any other, that the Afrikaans language has contributed to world language. It has entered into discourse everywhere, its impact has grown with the years. It is strange, this power of words over people, who invented them for their liberation, not for their enslavement.

2

The Banished

Personal Reflections

When *baaskap* gave way to apartheid, dissidents were dealt with by banishment to remote areas. The jails being full, mainly with pass offenders, recourse was made to South Africa's Siberias. Leaders into exile, the banished became the first of our martyrs; it is to these simple peasant folk that special homage is due for having spearheaded the revolt. For this reason they are given priority here. We are told – and history proves the point – that political power springs from the barrels of guns. Yet these peasants possessed no firearms whatsoever. Then what spurred them, what sustained them?

The truth is that they were driven by a despair so enormous as to be beyond our comprehension. It was a desperation born of a spellbinder's dream of the ultimate in apartheid, none less than Verwoerd's Bantustans.

I find it deplorable that apartheid supporters should blind themselves to the fact that tens of thousands of non-whites, mainly Africans, have been removed forcibly from ancestral lands with no more concern than is shown for cattle on its way to the slaughter house. Always the drive is in one direction, from fertile pastures to inhospitable, barren wastes. Renouncing all morality, Afrikanerdom has bulldozed its way to temporary land ownership, lasting enmity.

Increasingly there is talk of protest and of the right to protection for protestors. These peasants were accorded no rights, afforded no protection. It is said that our world accepts power, which is demonstrable, and rejects morality, the latter having no substance in fact. We can see how true this is by reference to parallel displays of political power in South Africa and on the West Bank of the Jordan, where Palestinian homes and vineyards have been bulldozed to make way for Jewish settlements. In both instances morality lies dormant. Nevertheless, for the final assessment we must await the verdict of history, the arbiter of a higher law than any to which mortals can lay claim.

Living in isolated communities, possessing no means of communication save the bush telegraph, the first to be dispossessed were ripe for the picking. The Government's task was easy. Methodically, armed forces were sent to crush resistance, demote tribal chiefs and headmen who were not compliant, promote stooges, banish the ringleaders. Each area of discontent could be dealt with singly, effectively. So much military efficiency was brought to bear that it was lauded by one of Britain's most illustrious wartime leaders, a vain and pompous little man, loud in his appraisal of the Afrikaner National Party and its version of the old divide and rule policy.

Field Marshall Lord Montgomery's fleeting visit to South Africa was the forerunner of a development having far reaching effect. Serving as praise-singer to Verwoerd, his 1959 journey was made at the behest of Sir Francis de Guingand, his World War II aide-de-camp. These two co-operated to promote the South Africa Foundation.

Monty's visit was a well laid scheme, a slickly organised commando raid to serve Dr Verwoerd's apartheid policy and shore up the sagging colonial system. Nothing was left to chance: there was no Bridge Too Far about this exercise. There was a beaming Monty meeting sychophantic Africans at the doorways to brand new homes, shaking hands with Ma and Pa, patting the heads of curly haired children, chatting about the good times ahead. He did not have time to probe deeply, but was impressed by all he saw. Of course. That is the object of conducted tours.

No reason was given as to why his stay was limited to a few minutes. Maybe, with time running short, there was no likelihood of the visitor straying beyond the last of the posh new houses into the first of the old shacks in shanty town.

A dutifully arranged Press conference followed, at which the knight errant sang his laudatory salutations, as was expected of him. What it all boiled down to was the exhortation 'Let's give it (the Bantustan policy) a try.' The same cry had been heard before, but coming from the lips of a renowned military strategist it sounded more essential than ever to curb all opposition.

Henceforth, all adverse criticism, all agitation, must be prevented. Verwoerd wanted TIME.

His successor, Vorster, was to take up the same theme; 'Give me six months', he pleaded. Always, power seekers want more power. Always, dictators need more time for their regimes. Always, oppressors look for ways and means to increase their hold upon subject masses. Time is the essential requirement. To gain it, Dr Verwoerd enlisted the services of a man whose conceit marked him as malleable to the division of South Africa into White and Black areas, the object being to secure the former at the expense of the latter. Or, if this failed, to split the country so decisively that it could not be reclaimed as a whole. The brilliance of this strategy lay in the fact that there was not to be a simple cleavage as between India and Pakistan. Instead there was to be one extensive, undivided white domain and a multiplicity of black squares and dots and rectangles, some of them mere tribal enclaves. By this subtlety the numerical superiority of the Africans would be set to nought. Only a few Quislings were required, and Time, which is not so readily available.

Montgomery's tremendous personal vanity was well known. What no one could have visualised was the extraordinary detachment of his narcissism in confrontation with the man whose genius had given rise to apartheid. Under the hypnotic gaze of Dr Verwoerd, the warlord's pride took leave of absence. Mesmerised by the master, captivated by his scheme, Monty capitulated.

Having sacrificed his vanity, he sought compensation and visualised it in the chance to balance his achievement in North Africa with an act of equal significance in South Africa. Having saved Britain, next he had to save her once great Empire from dissolution. Yearning to prove himself in peacetime as in war, he clutched at the opportunity to earn mention in the despatches of history as a man Successful in War, Successful in Peace. Mesmerised maybe, but victorious in the long run.

What he failed to understand was that decolonisation had set in irreversibly. No Dutch settler or visiting Englishman could deflect it from its course. Clearly, Montgomery overestimated his ability to reinforce the beleaguered racist outpost. Ah, vanity! What a shame to have tarnished his reputation in this inglorious manner.

In mitigation it can be said that if Lord Montgomery had not involved himself, some other volunteer would have come forward. In an overpopulated world there is no dearth of servile servers for any stint in life. A hangman is wanted, he comes from the shadows. A prison torturer is needed, he emerges from the slime. A praise-singer is required, a Field Marshall obliges.

For the oppressed there was to be further oppression. For the lonely there was to be increased loneliness. Areas already isolated were further isolated. With few exceptions, white South Africans did not know or care what happened in their name. They had the assurance that their future security was safe in the hands of a dependable father figure. In overseas markets, business with South Africa flourished; illustrious world figures spread the news that all was well.

Of the many peasant uprisings, the first took place 15 years before the Sharpeville massacre. The wave of unrest lasted 17 years. Witzieshoek, Marico, Zeerust, Pondoland, Sekhukuniland, these place-names represent tragedies untold. To stand firm in the face of mortal danger when unbefriended, with nothing save sticks and stones as weapons, with not a single scribe to tell of heroism, calls for courage. Or desperation bordering upon the suicidal.

To deprive people of freedom of movement while destroying their last vestige of security is to promote resistance, no matter what the odds. The history of Afrikanerdom should have warned of trouble in the offing. The Voortrekkers, once their political freedom had been assailed, sacrificed security of tenure for freedom of movement. The Great Trek resulted. Yet their descendants went out of their way to deny security *and* cut off freedom of movement to non-whites numbering millions. Why?

Was it a wrongful assessment of race and humanity that misled them? Or were they blinded by greed? Could they not see that a great spirit moves among peoples of the earth, from Viet Nam to Sekhukuniland?

In the lives of all there exists a yearning for security. Whether as feudalists or suburbanites, as desert nomads or settled agriculturalists, we look for a modicum of security. It constitutes a hunger. Similarly there is the desire for freedom of movement.

It constitutes a thirst. Occasionally the two are incompatible. Then it is that freedom of movement takes precedence. In this manner we are compelled to live our lives of contradiction, clinging to security, clutching at freedom. Few mortals succeed in achieving a balance between the two desirables. This being so, we should be careful not to deprive others of their security, or we may find ourselves bereft of freedom. Depriving others of their freedom, we may lose our own security. Life's balances are precariously poised.

The dispossessed blacks had no hope of success. Except through future generations. Meanwhile their lot was misery, a burgeoning sense of grievance, a loss of pride which weighed them down. There was nothing for their comfort save the spirit that springs from the soil, a strength which we, having divorced ourselves from the land to a large extent, fail to appreciate fully.

To their everlasting glory, these people of peasant stock were not stooges, willing to populate the parliaments of newly created Bantustans. Historians will be able to record next to nothing of the miseries and magnificence of those who opposed the warped and evil genius of the suave Hollander who master-minded separate development and called it apartheid.

My chance of setting poetry to political purpose came when Mrs Helen Joseph returned from her celebrated journey to centres of unrest from where rumours of heavy-handed repression emerged, rumblings of active resistance. Mrs Joseph's self-appointed task was to investigate, interview, report. Also to exhort and, through her presence, let the beleaguered populace know that someone cared. Most importantly, news must spread abroad of what was happening in Witzieshoek, Marico, Zeerust, Pondoland, Sekhukuniland. From the viewpoint of the armed police, she went to agitate.

Mrs Joseph was apprehended and her activities curtailed; as soon as could be arranged she was placed under house arrest. Free, in the sense that she was not jailed, but a prisoner in her own home. Years later she gained the distinction of remaining under house arrest for a record spell. Mrs Joseph was not able to publicise her findings, but fortunately I contacted her and was provided with information, some of which is embodied in the following poem dedicated to the first heroes of the revolution. As may be gathered, the words attributed to the three banished men are set down practically verbatim. All I have done is mould their words into a pattern of orderliness. My task was made easy because of the simplicity and sincerity of those concerned.

To provide a background of facts relating to the period of intensive unrest, a selection of newspaper reports are presented, together with excerpts from letters and unpublished articles passed on to me by Mrs Joseph. In themselves they afford a smattering of information concerning an heroic era that is all but lost to written history.

Background:

* 'If chiefs or headmen disagreed with Government policy, they were simply deposed or banished. Since the Nationalist Government came to power in 1948 no fewer than 132 chiefs have been banished to remote areas.' (Govan Mbeki at Rivonia Trial, May 1964. Sentenced to life imprisonment, initially to Robben Island. A friend of mine).

* Police seized a prominent, university-educated Pondo outside the Magistrate's Court in Bizana today, hustled him into a waiting Security Branch car and drove off to Kokstad, from where, it is believed, he will be banished to an undisclosed part of South Africa. (News report, Nov. 8th, 1960)

* 'We were at home when the agricultural officer came in a Government car and said to my husband, 'Stand up. Let's go.' They wanted to take me too, but when my husband knew that he was going to be banished, he would not let them take me. He said I must remain, for a soldier does not take his wife to war.' (Wife of banished man, Maema Matlala)

* 'What sort of prisoners are you? Prisoners go to jail and they come home again. But you don't come home.' (Extract from letter written by tribal African to her banished husband)

* 'An agricultural officer came on a motor bike and told my husband to go to the police station at Sandfontein. I do not remember what year this was. He was taken away by train and I did not get a letter from him all the years afterwards until the day when he walked into the house. I did not know where he had been and I thought it was a ghost and I got a shock. This was on a Monday in June 1961. He collapsed onto the floor, and

11

then he struggled to his feet and asked, 'How are you? How are the children?' He said he was well, but he wasn't well and he fell down again. He lay in bed for a week and then he died. He did not speak again after that first day.' (Statement from wife of banished man)

** Excerpts from letters and notes provided by Mrs Helen Joseph before she was placed under house arrest:

* I knew something of the difficulties under which these people lived, but until I saw them I did not understand the stark reality. I was shocked.

* There are no words which can really tell how deeply these banished people have suffered and yet the abiding memory is not of pity but inspiration, for the courage of these lonely exiles is undimmed, their spirit is unbreakable. They are amongst the greatest heroes of our struggle.

* They put on their brightest headscarves and their gayest beads, but as one by one they told their tragic stories, the sky seemed less blue and the gay colours served only to deepen the lines of sorrow on their dark faces. Sometimes the tears rolled down their cheeks as they told how their husbands had been taken away so long ago. Of them all, only one had returned.

* In November 1957, when he was at the Royal Kraal in Sekhukuniland, Kgagudi Maredi's banishment order was brought by a Colonel of the S.A. Police, escorted by 13 vanloads of armed police. Together with his cousin Kgagudi Marutenyane, he refused at first to move a foot from his land, and a fight with the police followed. 'The police knocked me about, hitting me very badly. I was bleeding. Then we were both put in leg irons and handcuffs. We were taken like this on a lorry to the police station at Skoonard, and then in a closed van all the way to the Ciskei. The leg irons were not taken off until we reached Kieskamahoek, where we left Marutenyane and I was brought to this place, after sleeping one night in Kingwilliamstown jail. But I did not have any medical attention for my wounds.

A year later, Maredi was allowed to go back to Sekhukuniland, for a limited period and on condition that he did not hold or attend any meetings, and other such restrictions. After one year, with others who had been banished at the same time, he was called to Pretoria to the Secretary for Native Affairs, and there he was told that he was No. 1 Agitator, and must be sent back to Kingwilliamstown. He was not allowed to return to Sekhukuniland to collect his belongings or say goodbye to his wife.

* I had seen Maredi's wife in far off Sekhukuniland. Lonely and anxious, she remains with her two young daughters. Her memories of the banishments of her husband are bitter and full of grief. On neither occasion was he allowed to come home to tell her of his banishment. She had to learn the news from others, and wait for word from him.

* We have a duty, a debt to these banished people. For many years they were alone, forgotten, and it is only in the last three years that committees have been set up to bring them assistance, human contact. There is much for us to do for them now, but most of all these lonely people must be assured that they shall never again be forgotten.

* . . . the cover has been ripped off and the festering evil of this banishment system shown for what it is, a slow torture of the soul, a living death. It is a crime against humanity and a savage violation of the rule of law, of fundamental human rights.

* No longer can this Government be allowed to hide this shameful secret. For not one of these men has ever been charged in any court of law for the crime, if crime there be, which led to his banishment. Not one has ever been given the chance to defend himself, to prove his innocence.

** *Looking back:* 'No freeman shall be arrested or detained in prison, or deprived of his freehold, or outlawed or banished or in any way molested; and we shall not set forth against him unless by the lawful judgement of his peers and by the law of the land.' (Magna Carta, 1215)

** Note from Mrs Helen Joseph, Sept. 18th 1962, after poem *The Banished* had been published:

Stephen Nkadimeng's words are correctly reported. He stood beside the car as we were leaving and said, 'I am alright. Nkadimeng is not worried. The struggle of my people goes on.'

And indeed that is what he wanted to know from us more than anything else. Were the people getting stronger, was the Government getting weaker? He did not dwell at all on his own lonely, dreary life, and this is what I found everywhere, the banished people do not cry for pity. Their thoughts are turned outwards, to their own people and to their homes. Their dignity and pride is immense; it is not a meek beaten acceptance, but a strong will to survive, to wait until the day when they will go home again.

** *Author's concluding note:*
For a while I contrived to send letters and parcels to Nkadimeng, redirected from the nearest post office. Then, inevitably, the end came. I do not know how, but with lines of communication difficult at the best of times, our tenuous bond was broken. Likewise I lost touch with Helen Joseph.

Shortly after publication of *The Banished*, it was declared illegal to quote any banned or banished person, any named communist, anyone imprisoned, exiled, placed under house arrest or otherwise restricted. In short, anyone who dare oppose apartheid, the latest experiment in the ages old policy of divide and rule. No matter what is said to the contrary, censorship was in operation as long ago as the early 1960s.

THE BANISHED

Huddled against roofless walls they lie
   dispirited, broken as the walls.
Perhaps, on the morrow they will die
   or, living, will not heed what fate befalls.
Vaguely existing like unwilling shadows,
   voiceless and echoless and impotent,
   the blood in their veins is a stream that flows
   only downward, without power of ascent.
Titanic longings make their only prayer
   a prayer for death. They have surrendered
   all but the broken body, and despair
   is the only hope since God has not heard
   their frequent pleas.
               Perhaps death, relenting,
   will accept them soon. Otherwise the tide
   changes not for them; nor does the sun bring
   seasonal plenty. How can they hold pride,
   being hungry? Or know of further pain,
   being full of it? How is beauty known,
   or love, or peace, unless they come again?
And how is kindliness or mercy shown
   by avenging angels?
               Our apathy
   imprisons us, our guilt walls us in. Fear
   bars our way, changes light into dark. See
   the accused are free.
               Search, they are not here.
And so, wearied, we leave them where they lie,
   dispirited and broken till they die.

*   *   *   *

Voice of Stephen Nkadimeng, banished from Sekhukuniland:

> Except for this!
> Nkadimeng is not afraid.
> Nkadimeng is all right.
> He is beyond hurt
>   but not beyond caring.
> How are my people?
> Is the Government weakening,
>   are my people getting stronger?
> Nkadimeng speaks from afar, from the wilderness
>   but not from an empty heart.
> There is much time for thought here,
>   but little does Nkadimeng think about himself.
> His thoughts are not here,
>   they are with his people.
> Should you think of me, then think of this:
>   Nkadimeng is not worried.
> The struggle of my people goes on.

*   *   *   *

Voice of Kenneth Mosenyi, banished from Zeerust:

> This is what matters, bravery.
> This is what counts, courage.
> Mosenyi has both,
>   enough and to spare.
> A Government official says
>   I should write to the Minister in Pretoria,
>   asking to be sent home.
> Me, Mosenyi the militant! Ask? Plead?
>   And lose honour?
> The Minister put me here. It is not for me
>   to go on my knees and ask
>   for freedom as a favour.
> No, I shall not heed the voice of the tempter
>   though I be promised a kingdom.
> Here is my kingdom, here,
>   in the heart of Mosenyi.

*   *   *   *

Voice of Kgagudi Maredi, banished from Sekhukuniland:

> The men in Pretoria
>   call me Agitator. Number One Agitator!
> Yes, I agitate, but not for myself.
> I agitate for freedom, and freedom
>   is in unity. It is not
>   a thing apart, a selfish whim.
> Without freedom
>   my people cannot work for the world
>   – only for their masters.
> Without freedom
>   where is tomorrow's yield, the harvest
>   or the thanksgiving?
> If this is the language of agitation
>   then Maredi remains
>   what he was in Sekhukuniland.

3

Amandla, Strength

When majority rule takes over, as it must, I hope it will be borne in mind that South African Indians bore the brunt of Verwoerdian policy from the start. In particular they suffered under the Group Areas Act, which empowers the Government to evict non-whites and let in land hungry whites. As a defenceless minority group the Indians were vulnerable and were singled out for victimisation of an especially savage nature. I saw it as neither *klein* (petty, small) apartheid nor *groot* (big, great) apartheid. It deserved a name of its own. I called it brute apartheid.

Through Press reports my attention was drawn to the case of Nana Sita, a disciple of Gandhian passive resistance who had fought every attempt at forcible removal from his property on the outskirts of Pretoria, using legal court procedure. Covetously, the ruling whites wanted it for themselves, preferring to be free from the stigma of a single non-white in their midst, let alone an Indian trader. Though acquired many years before, the property had to be relinquised, though it was preferable for the take-over to be negotiated through lawful channels so as not to negate Christian principles. What better for the purpose than the Group Areas Act?

Ensuing legalities proved so costly that Nana Sita was broken monetarily. His crippling arthritis, which made a walking aid essential, broke him physically. Only his moral values remained unimpaired. As he pointed out in a letter which I treasure to this day; 'The road to Cross of Calvary is full of thorns and very hazardous, but those who wish to stand up against injustices and oppression have no choice but to tread on that road and to willingly undergo all sufferings and make sacrifices until the oppressor is obliged to change his evil ways.'

As a man of moral integrity, Nana Sita had to make his stand, costly though it proved in terms of cash outlay and physical wellbeing. As a disciple of Gandhi he had to make use of passive resistance, which proved so effective against comparatively mild British rule in India. Against hardened, unrelenting Afrikaner administration it was of no avail. All the same, there was no choice but to tread that road, and to Nana Sita we are indebted for imparting to the armed struggle a certain morality at an early stage. This is important to those who, later, are left with no alternative but to take up arms.

Aghast at the treatment of this courageous Indian, a South African of longer residence than Dr Verwoerd, I contrived to draw attention to his plight through the medium of a political power poem first published, appropriately, on Human Rights Day, 1963. As pointed out at the time; 'There are few left now, free to speak openly, able to speak clearly, with sufficient inner resolve to speak fearlessly.'

As with *The Banished*, an historical background was provided, made up of news items appearing between 1960 and 1963. These are retained in their original context, serving to highlight the ruthlessness of an oppressive regime which sought to deprive others of their basic rights by any means available. They make the law of the jungle appear tame by comparison.

The Mounting Agony:

* The 850 Indians of Pietersburg, most of whom are descended from settlers who trekked to the town by ox-wagon in 1884, have been ordered out of their homes and shops to barren veld about two miles from the town. (News report, March 1960)

* 'No one knows what a terrible thing this is till it happens to you. Everyone goes to bed at night and wakes up in the morning asking; "What shall I do? Where can I go? Cannot anyone help me?" ' (Old Indian shopkeeper, one of 50 families ordered by Group Areas inspectors to get out of their homes at Sea Point)

* 'Now it is paid for, now I must go. How can I start all over again?' (63-year-old widow telling of 30-year struggle to pay for a home in South End, Port Elizabeth)

* 'I will continue to oppose the evil of this Act as long as I live.' (Nana Sita of Hercules, Pretoria)

* While thousands of whites celebrated the second anniversary of the Republic in a gay and carefree mood, Indians from all parts of the Eastern Transvaal gathered at Bethal to pray for help against the Group Areas Act. (News report, June 1963)

* At the inquest on two men, it was stated that they committed suicide because they were ordered to move under the Group Areas Act. One of the men left a note blaming the Act for his death. (News report, 1963)

* Bougaardt complained that the Group Areas Board wanted to give him next to nothing for his property. When he spoke about Group Areas he cried a lot. In the top pocket of Bougaardt's jacket was a scrap of brown paper. On it was written in red ink; 'Group Areas is the cause of doing away with my life.' (News report, January 1960)

* S.A. House of Assembly, 1960. Mr J. F. Naude; 'I am getting tired of the attitude of the Indians.'

Background: Concerning a girl since tortured while in police custody.

The sister of one of three prisoners, Miss Shantie Naidoo, shouted out to the men as they were about to be driven away in the police van, 'Amandla.'
Col. J. Wright, standing a yard in front of her, turned round and said; 'Why do you use a native word? You women don't understand these things!'
Miss Naidoo; 'It means Strength.'
Col. Wright to the policemen; 'Hurry up with that van.'

AMANDLA, STRENGTH!

Amandla, Strength!
We must have strength twofold,
Strength within and strength without,
Strength in bone and muscle, nerve and sinew,
Strength in something more, something surer,
Strength in something lasting, something constant,
Steadfast strength that does not wilt or wither,
    does not fade or tire, bend or break with age.

Amandla, Strength!
We must have strength twofold,
Strength for today and some left over,
Strength in the hour of need and for the waiting moment,
Strength for ourselves and some for others,
Strength for the family and some for the nation,
Self-sufficiency and a surplus offering
    that adds a cubit to humanity's stature.

Amandla, Strength!
We must have strength twofold,
Strength to sever the bonds of servitude,
Strength to rise in freedom, so to serve,
Strength for survival and some for progress,
Strength for the righting of wrongs (brave for the while)
Strength for upholding of right (to be true always)
    come the good fight and the peace that follows.

Amandla, Strength!
We must have strength twofold,
Strength to withhold the inner plaguing doubt,
Strength to withstand the tempter lurking without,
Strength to grow in full image and likeness,
Strength to remain humble always,
Disdaining privilege, the tempter's guilefulness
    known for what it is, and not unknown, the price.

Amandla, Strength!
We must have strength twofold,
Strength for unsullied days, redoubled in crisis years,
Strength to confront the aggressor, the oppressor and not faint,
Strength to outvie banishment, imprisonment and not quail,
Strength for the torment, the prison insult, the jailer's jest,
Strength under whiplash, in cells of solitude,
    that we may endure to the end and not be broken.

*   *   *   *

How not to tire, where to find strength?
Passing stranger, tell us
Where lies strength, the strength twofold,
What is its source, when to arrive?

Strength is here and now, it lies within, without;
Twofold is its source, in us its meeting point.
Alone, we summon up a fraction of it – half at most;
Allying ourselves, we gain its fullest measure.

It lies within, and yet its source evades
    the deepest cut of the surgeon's blade;
It lies without, and yet its source eludes
    the farthest probe in space.

Its power is in our hands, yet when we clench our fists
    we lose it.
Its might is in our minds, but when we steel our thoughts
    we lose it.
Its joy is in our hearts, and when we harden them
        we lose it.

Our strength is here and now, within, without,
Like treasure trove that waits the finding;
    we still our raging breasts and gain it.

4

The Martyrs

Personal Reflections

Seldom can it be said of a living man that he is a martyr. As a rule, this highest of honours awaits the dead. Yet for my political development I was indebted to a man whom I recognised as a martyr in the making. This was Govan Mbeki, an exceptional man as befits an exception to a general rule. Though incarcerated on Robben Island for many years, penal servitude does not make of him a criminal, especially in this age when prisoners of conscience are so numerous. On the contrary, intense incarceration, along with an assassin's bullet or a hangman's noose, acts as an agent of martyrdom.

After his capture at Rivonia, a suburb of Johannesburg, and his evidence at the momentous Rivonia Trial, Govan was sentenced to life imprisonment. He was sent to Robben Island, and in effect he died on the day he was transported to the low offshore island which is visible from Cape Town on a clear day. With not the remotest chance of escape, nor any hope of reprieve, he warrants his martyrdom now. If white, and a hardened, callous criminal, he could have anticipated a sizeable remission of sentence. As a political activist, and black, he must expect his life sentence to mean precisely that; loss of liberty until death, never again to be a free man.

Not that he was ever really free. His family history of oppression included his father, a chief by birth, born in the Nqumakwe District of the Transkei, though he was reduced to headman because of his opposition to the rising tide of apartheid legislation. Still refusing to bow to Government coercion, he was deposed.

Govan's political career began in the depression years of the 1930s. Scholastically brilliant, he set out to be a teacher, the only career available to him as a black man. To be true to himself and his upbringing, Govan had to look upon teaching as

23

a vocation enabling him to reach out to his pupils politically. For his insubordination he suffered dismissal from one Government-subsidised school after another until forced to take up junior positions in the Transkei, there to be hounded further, though he was Transkeian born. Finding it impossible to remain in teaching, he accepted a Port Elizabeth post as regional editor of *New Age*. When this publication was banned, he transferred to its successor, *Spark*. When this was banned under restrictive law introduced for the purpose, making it impossible to continue publishing the same tabloid newspaper under a new name, Govan was out of work. Thereafter all avenues were blocked to him unless he should lower his sights so far as to become a house boy, garden hand or messenger. In this manner, criminals are made. Or martyrs.

There existed one form of escape, though not from martyrdom. He could go underground. This he did.

Before judging any man, let alone censoring him, we need to take into account his background. As a man of character and learning, what else could Govan have done?

His mother was the daughter of a Methodist minister, so it followed that he was brought up in the Christian faith, which he abandoned reluctantly. Or did religion abandon him? Leaving the Transkei for Port Elizabeth, he had to say goodbye to wife and family. This was due to the fact that Govan had not worked continuously with one Port Elizabeth employer for a minimum of ten years, an impossible demand. As a result he did not qualify for a rented house and could not have his family with him. This is one way in which marriages are made fragile and family ties are broken for non-whites by law makers who proclaim themselves religious and do all in their power to ensure the sanctity of marriage for themselves.

As a result of his wide knowledge of Transkeian affairs, coupled with his purposefulness and persistence, Govan gained recognition as a key member of the African National Congress in the Port Elizabeth regional area, where he served on the national executive from 1956. With the banning of the ANC he became a member of the National High Command of *Umkhonto we Sizwe*, Spear of the Nation.

Umkhonto was doomed, and so was Govan. Clearly to me at the time, confrontation with Government forces held no chance of success. Pathetically, tragically, a show had to be made as a gesture of defiance, a sacrifice for the altar of the gods. The pathway to freedom is never easy, and in this instance it was too much to hope that the first organised assault upon the citadel of Afrikanerdom should succeed.

Govan was declared a communist, but his listing as such was a lie at the time. Only later did he turn to communism, impelled by frustration. It was as though the National Party, bitterly anticommunist, acted as an agent of communism, gave rise to it, prospered it. A kind of death wish operated, with apartheid turning upon itself, sowing the seeds of its own destruction.

My introduction to Govan came indirectly through my wife, who initiated a meeting with a prominent New Brighton clergyman and myself. Through channels unbeknown, he directed me to a 'leading African nationalist', who turned out to be Govan Mbeki. The clergyman did not impress me. Too late, it was hinted that he was a police informer, of whom there were many in those dark days. Looking back, I feel certain that he informed against me. A shifty-eyed fellow, he was at loggerheads with Govan politically, so why had he made the introduction if not to betray me? Simultaneously he may have sought to ingratiate himself with African patriots. We were to meet once more, at his wife's funeral, and I remember glancing up to find him watching me with furtive gaze when his head should have been bowed in prayer. Judas, Judas!

My initial meeting with Govan came shortly after his release from prison on a trumped-up charge that was widely publicised. He was jailed while awaiting trial (a normal procedure) but the case against him was so glaringly at fault that it was thrown out of court when a State witness was proved an unmitigated liar. Then it came to light that he had been set up by the police and stood to gain monetarily as a result of his treachery. Cases of this kind were frequent, and it was not uncommon for gross misrepresentations of justice to result, with innocent wretches paying the price. On this occasion the duplicity of the police and their accomplice did not succeed, but only because the evidence of the false witness was so palbably untrue as to be inadmissible.

Surprises were in store for me once I had located the building and been ushered into a bare barn of an office. I have heard tell of fascist dictators seated at raised desks at the end of long approaches over deep-pile carpets. Visitors must be made to feel small and unimportant. What a contrast this scene presented. A couple of strides and I halted before a desk draped with a rough blanket. There was a typewriter and two hard chairs devoid of cushions. Three walls were bare, the fourth had pinned to it a newspaper clipping of Lumumba, the murdered Congolese leader, his hands manacled behind his back, a look of dread in his upturned eyes. A few minutes later and he was dead.

I thought I was alone. Then I caught sight of a man hunched beneath the blanketed desk. I waited, perplexed. Presently a man's head appeared; he was on the point of finishing a telephone conversation. How odd. Replacing the receiver and struggling free, the man rose to shake hands. Meetings and greetings. Many have I made, but none more strange than this. Why the telephone on the floor? Why the covering blanket? An aspiring politician, there was much for me to learn concerning the politics of the hunted.

Rather older than me, Govan was almost as tall, and like me greying, quietly spoken, undemonstrative. However he was much more mature, much more a man of this world. Early in our conversation I asked what sort of treatment he had received while in prison awaiting trial, with bail refused because of his political stature. He paused before answering. Then in his quiet manner he said, 'If you mean did they illtreat me physically, the answer is No. But there are other ways of achieving the same result. I was kept in solitary confinement, and in a number of ways I was made to feel like an animal. My lavatory bucket was kept inside my cell and was not emptied until it overflowed. No toilet paper was supplied. My food was slops. No chance was lost to make me feel less than human.'

My admiration for Govan grew. I am not easy to impress as a rule, but within minutes it became obvious that here was a dependable man. He was like a sage of old, inwardly assured, exuding wisdom. He was like a good mountain guide, unobtrusive, never doubting the way ahead, infinitely knowledgeable of his territory. I trusted him instinctively. And strangely for a man whose liberty was endangered, who found it necessary to crouch under a desk while using the telephone, he returned my trust.

I am not one of those gifted chroniclers capable of instant, total recall of conversations, especially of this kind, which spring from the heart and mind and are not intended for the record. Suffice it to say that interest did not flag at any stage as we covered a wide range of related topics, with Govan the master and me his understudy. My mentor knew of me through my no-nonsense political writings, which followed his own line of thought precisely. Otherwise he may not have been so ready to receive me in what were to prove his last few days of freedom. To his credit he made no attempt to influence me. Perhaps he sensed that he need not try, for it must have been apparent to him, as to me, that we agreed on nearly every aspect of the involved political situation, with its accent upon race and colour. For my part, it was pleasing to receive confirmation, to learn that my independent line of thought was so advanced. He did not change me or my mode of thought, but by affording the benefit of his wider experience he convinced me of the rightness of my stand. This was my greatest need, not flattery but honest appraisal.

When I invited Govan to my home in Redhouse he declined graciously but firmly. 'Members of the Special Branch follow my movements closely', he explained. 'It would not be right for me to be seen in Redhouse, let alone at your home'. He spoke quietly as usual, making no attempt to dramatise the situation. It did not dawn upon me until later that he was saving me from what may have been the consequences of my folly, from constant surveillance which he knew so well and I knew nothing of – though I was to experience it shortly, the growing certainty of being watched, followed at a distance, accompanied by the long shadow of the law. Through the years I have thanked this considerate man a thousand times for shielding me the way he did.

Govan remains a good man in my opinion, despite his life sentence. Not saintly after the manner of Gandhi, but honest, uncomplicated, fearless and utterly incorruptible. Not a man for the torture chamber. I do not think he would yield under the most drastic of pressures. He sought no glory for himself. He accepted it as his duty to speak for the voiceless masses, that they might be freed from racist oppression and accorded a say in their own affairs. His father, the deposed chief, had bred in him a sense of obligation.

He could have joined his son in England if he had wished. Existing escape routes were open to him, mostly leading north to Botswana. Already a number of leaders had gone into exile, both ANC and PAC. There was a faction who considered it best to go while the going was good. They saw it as their duty to leave in order to benefit their cause abroad, establishing relations with friendly powers. The beleaguered folk must know that they were not alone in their struggle. If resistance cannot be made from within, it needs to be organised from without. Those who left did not go to prosper themselves; they perceived a greater use abroad, spreading their talents, not wasting them in prison. There were others who saw it as their duty to remain. Govan was one. Steadfastly he refused to go.

Either way sacrifice was invoked. We should not censure those who left, we should not be critical of those who remained. Ultimately it will be seen as fortunate that some were destined to go, others to stay.

What surprised me was that Govan uttered not one word of recrimination against his oppressors. He was not embittered. Nor did he complain, though he worked under utmost difficulty, the extent of which beggars description. His office had been raided so often that scarcely anything remained. Most journalists sit at desks cluttered with sheets of paper, scribble pads, newspaper cuttings, magazine articles, pens, pencils; normally there are files and reference books, dictionaries, maps and atlasses. Govan had to make do with the barest essentials, a typewriter, and on the floor, the telephone. But no telephone directory. Every essential number had to be committed to memory. No back issues of the banned *New Age* could be kept. Editing under difficulties. A minimal freedom, a hunted, almost animal existence.

In one respect Govan was lucky. For a black man to occupy a building within city environs was exceptional. His office was situated near the Law Courts, while immediately opposite was the fine, modern office of the Commandant of Police, a portly Afrikaner who bore an implacable racist hate. North End was not one of the most salubrious of suburbs, but was due to be upgraded. Already zoned "White", it was a matter of weeks only before Govan and his staff could be sent packing. Meanwhile, when not at their desks, the two protagonists stood

before their office windows and glowered at one another across
intervening Main Street. Observing them, a close friend of
mine told how Govan's face was serene, bearing no trace of malice, whereas the countenance of his oppressor was filled with
malevolence.

There was a change in Govan's appearance when I called to
see him a fortnight later. He was distraught, as though something weighed upon his mind. There was a secret which had to
be kept and it imposed a burden. Despite this, we chatted ami-
cably and there was the same master-disciple relationship as
before. In Govan Mbeki I had found my political mentor. Also,
I recognised in him the makings of a martyr. I must have been
the last to meet him openly. At my next call he was gone.

As on the two previous occasions I was greeted by an attrac-
tive young woman who recognised me at once, her face
beaming. Seated on a bare wooden bench was a bearded African, surely a stalwart of the resistance movement. He
impressed me as an elder statesman, dignified and wise, a man
to be trusted; too old to be jailed, too stoical for the torture
chamber. Later generations should hesitate before claiming
betrayal by their elders. A woman who may have been his wife
sat beside him. Solid as rocks in their convictions they must
have been, or they could not have exposed themselves in this
manner, in a place raided so frequently by the police. I recall
them to mind often, with anxiety. My own dedication owes
much to them.

Without waiting to be asked, the young girl informed me;
'Govan is gone.'

'Gone, but where?'

'Underground.'

It was a simple statement of fact, unembellished.

All three disavowed any knowledge as to Govan's whereabouts, and I believed them. Typically, he had left no information which might have been extorted in solitary confinement, or
worse, under physical torture, which leaves its associated pain
arising from the embarrassment of betrayal.

Poor Govan. His life had been a round of deprivation. His
tribal authority had been taken from him. He had lost his belief
in a deity. (Had he abandoned God, or had God abandoned
him?) He had been forced to turn from teaching. Under duress

he had relinquished his former liberalism. His belief in non-violence had been shattered. He had been made to live apart from his wife and family. As a last sacrifice there was his limited freedom. An age-old tragedy was being enacted, and only the final scene had to be played to its bitter end.

Critics are apt to claim that it is wrong for a writer to show emotionalism. It represents bad form. Those who think along these lines uncompromisingly must be case hardened, or their experiences of life are so limited as to stunt their feelings. It may have softened them if they had been with me as I peered into Govan's old office as though seeking visual proof of what I had been told. The only evidence of his former occupancy was the telephone lying on the floor and the photo of Patrice Lumumba, still in place on the wall. Initially shocked, then rising from a state of misery, I grew angry with those in authority. It is people of irrational fear who are at fault, not emotionalism.

They fear that to give a little may lead to giving more. They use fear as a tool, set it to work, and it works to their destruction. Better by far to feel emotion and be freed from fear.

In Govan's last public utterance he declared; 'We, black and white, who have respect for human dignity, must make a bold stand. We have a double duty to perform. On the one hand we must save South Africans from the corrosive effects on their moral fibre of having to defend a system for which there is not a shred of moral justification. We must protect them from having to administer the inhuman laws that flow from it. On the other hand we have to save the victim, the African, from the bitterness which springs from the degredation and humiliation accompanying the application of these laws.'

Are these the words of a terrorist? Or of a martyr in the making?

My next visit to Govan's empty barn was a memorable occasion. Bounding up the rickety wooden stairway two steps at a time, as is my habit, I realised my folly too late. In the back of my mind there lurked the thought that, with Govan gone, there would be no further raids. I should have known better, and climbed the stairs cautiously. With Govan underground, a closer watch than ever could be expected in case the missing man tried to contact his former colleagues. With reckless abandonment I carried on as far as a swing door at the top. Then yanking it open I almost fell into the arms of two hulking members of the Special Branch. It is difficult to say who was the more surprised. With my propensity for preoccupation of thought I can be slow on the uptake, but this was one of my brighter moments. Reacting spontaneously, I whirled on my heels and fled precipitately while trying to look as though I had blundered into the wrong building.

I had not seen these two men before, but was in no doubt as to their calling. Apart from an animal instinct which gave warning, I had evolved so far as to be able to pick out members of the Special Branch as though by scent. In addition to their unmistakable physical attributes, they are look-alikes, all stolid, emotionless, ponderous of movement unless quickened by a crisis. They do not possess bright shining faces and are by no means gifted with sparkling intellect and ready wit. They operate in pairs as a rule. Examine a photograph of rugby football players piling into a scrum and you will see their counterparts. Good at their rough and tumble sport, all cast in the same mould, lacking finesse.

Going down the stairs three at a bound did not take long; at street level it seemed expedient to ease my pace to that of a trained athlete at the start of a short sprint. Rounding the first corner I eased further to a swift canter, my heart pounding. I was not being followed, if only because the two Special Branch men were not slim enough or quick enough off the mark to give chase. They had no need to worry; time was on their side, together with all the machinations of the law. Common criminals may slip the net occasionally, political offenders seldom if ever.

Despite this near brush with the political arm of the law, I returned on the following Saturday morning. There was the desire to know what had transpired after my hurried flight of the previous occasion. Danger beckoned too, as it does to the adventurous and to those who would be their own executioners. A concession was made in taking more care. Adapting myself to the call for caution, I tiptoed upstairs, schooling myself to rely upon visual stimulus rather than animal instinct. It would not do to turn and run a second time. So, varying my tactics, I decided to play it cool if the necessity arose. Fortunately it did not. There was no raid in progress.

The same trusty stalwarts were there, defiant as ever, arousing my admiration as before. It demands courage of the highest order to defy the Special Branch, with dire penalties for losers. To climb a Himalayan peak, to drive a Formula I racing car, to ride in a T.T. race in competition with the world's fastest and most fearless superstars, these pursuits call for courage of an exceptional kind. But it is blind courage, with fame and fortune as spurs. Resistance to racial politics calls for courage of a higher order, calm and clear. The penalty is not a quick death but incarceration for life, with a visit or two to the torture chamber.

The receptionist, with only caretaker duties left to her, confirmed the visit of the two Special Branch men. She, and the elderly couple, had been questioned as to my identity and the reason for my visit.

'We told them we did not know your name, and that you had called to see Govan.'

Undoubtedly the Special Branch men knew all they wanted to know already, for their efficiency had increased immeasurably. They had learnt the techniques of interrogation to the extent that they were exporting their know-how. Stolid maybe, but they knew the rules of rugby football and were well versed in the "investigative techniques" of racist policy.

Nothing more was heard of Govan until there came the shattering news of his capture at Lilliesleaf Farm, in the select suburb of Rivonia. There followed the sensational "window dressing" trial which attracted worldwide attention, as was intended, for the western world of white supremacy must have displayed before it the trappings of African nationalism, presented as part of a communist plot. The display became known as the Rivonia Trial. By design it led to life imprisonment for Govan Mbeki and six others captured with him, including Walter Sisulu, Raymond Mhlaba and Ahmed Kathrada, a South African Indian activist. Also Nelson Mandela, Elias Motsoaledi and Andrew Mlangeni were charged with them.

The prisoners were allowed to testify, and each acquitted himself well, no one more so than Govan Mbeki, perhaps the most deeply contemplative and articulate of them all. So capably did the accused espouse their cause that never again were African nationalists afforded the opportunity to address an open court. The Judge President said in his summing up, 'I doubt very much whether the motives for their crimes were as altruistic as they would have the court believe.' Mr Justice De Wet's words found ready acceptance among apartheid supporters. They had the ring of authority. But did they ring true?

While accepting that, in saints and sinners alike, self-interest and self-sacrifice are difficult to distinguish and almost impossible to separate, I believe they rang hollowly. Speaking for Govan, he was so much in command of himself and so considerate of others, that any accuser would need to look high, not low, to service in the interest of others, not to motives shallow and mean. Gifted with intelligence and natural charm, he was no crafty, cunning criminal. He knew what was in store for him, as did Jesus Christ, Thomas A'Beckett, Saint Paul and Gandhiji. He knew the slender chance of success for active resistance movements bereft of external aid. But like his father he had tasted great persecution, and he knew that the old fetters must be broken; or, defeated in war, his people would be defeated in peacetime, and thus would have no pride remaining. The call was for sacrifice, the only means whereby suffering can be ameliorated, reduced to a tolerable level. It fell upon his generation, specifically himself and his co-conspirators, to set in motion the chain of sacrifice, that others might have life more abundantly. The temptation to slip the tightening net of the law had existed but so had the call to duty, with its essential sacrifice. Govan and those charged with him were subject to a higher law than was their judge, who so derided them.

Mr Justice De Wet's summing up may have represented the truth as he saw it, but did he view the circumstances as an impartial judge or as a racist, a National Party supporter, a man who could be relied upon to reach a conclusion comforting to those who had appointed him? Was Govan as bad as Mr Justice De Wet tried to make out? Was he a man of corrupt motivation? Was he a communist and a criminal, as though the one must be the other? Or was he a man meant to be a martyr? The answer can be left to history, a ponderous but impartial judge.

Life's work ended for Govan and his associates when they were transported to Robben Island, there to break stones to no

purpose save to satisfy the vanity of their captors and ring out a
message of faint hope:

> Through sacrifice the gods are appeased; this is
> the logic of martyrdom. By way of selfless
> endeavour a cause is prospered and the way made
> ready for the concerted efforts of others.
> Martyrdom marks an end and a new beginning.
> It provides a genesis for change in a situation
> of dangerously thwarted change. It honours a
> people who have been deprived of honour.
> Martyrdom serves as a beacon, lighting the way
> for followers. It signifies, 'This much we can
> do for you and no more; the rest is up to you.'

Background:

* 'There was nothing left to us but to suffer.' (Elias Motsoaledi
at Rivonia Trial)

* Pravda, on Rivonia Trial sentences: 'Executioners acting in
the role of jurors found people quilty whose names are for Africans bound up with their hopes for a better future.'

* 'The tree of liberty has not grown from the conference table.
It will grow only if watered by the blood of martyrs.' (Soweto
student)

* 'This is now a life and death struggle and there are people
who have put sufficient value into the cause to die for it.'
(Neville Curtis, S. African exile)

* 'As a man, Nelson is passionate, emotional, sensitive,
quickly stung to bitterness and retaliation by insult and
patronage. He has a natural air of authority. He cannot help
magnetizing a crowd: he is commanding with a tall, handsome
bearing; trusts and is trusted by the youth, for their impatience
reflects his own. He is dedicated and fearless. He is a born mass
leader.' (Oliver Tambo)

* 'My husband is the same man who was sentenced in June
1964, tremendous spirit. Absolutely fantastic.' (Winnie Mandela, 1982)

* 'If 20,000 of us have to be killed so that 20 million of us can be free, it will still be a price worth paying.' (Soweto student)

* 'There are nearly 2,500 political prisoners in our prisons. These men and women are not criminals but the staunchest opponents of apartheid.' (Abram Fischer, Q.C., 1962)

* 'Black consciousness has permeated the whole of the black community. The spirit is there. To kill the spirit you will have to kill the people.' (Bishop Manus Buthelezi)

* 'The purpose of black consciousness is to provide some kind of hope. . . . We have to rewrite our history and produce in it the heroes that formed the core of our resistance to the white invaders.' (Steven Biko)

THE MARTYRS

   1.   Mangaleso Robert Sobukwe . . .

     You stand accused of incitement
       to commit an offence
       against the Pass Laws.
     How do you plead,
       Guilty or Not Guilty?

     Guilty in the eyes of our oppressors,
       though history, which takes a longer view,
       a wiser, wider and stronger view,
       will proclaim my innocence.
     We would have failed in our duty
       had we not made our contribution
       to the nation's struggle.
     History will find its own path;
       we do not count as individuals.

     My people,
       pray not for me
       but for our oppressors.

       *   *   *   *

2.   Rohinhlala Nelson Mandela . . .

You stand accused of sabotage.
How do you plead,
    bearing in mind that I will not tolerate
    political speeches in a court of law?

I do not deny that I planned sabotage.
I planned it
    not in a spirit of recklessness
    but in calm and sober assessment
    after many years of oppression
    and tyranny of my people.
We had to accept inferiority
    or fight against it.
We chose the latter course.
If this be violence, nevertheless
    I will still be moved.

To put an end to domination,
    This was my act of dedication.
It is an idea I hope to see realised
    but, my lord, it is an idea
    for which I am prepared to die.

My people,
    pray not for me
    but for our adjudicators.

      ★   ★   ★   ★

3.   Govan Mbeki . . .

You stand accused of sabotage.
It is said that you are ruthless.
Why do you transgress?

I feel no moral guilt.
We, both black and white,
    who have respect for human dignity,
    must make a stand freely, fearlessly.
I have spoken the truth on many occasions
    in order to expose evil.
If one can be said to transgress
    on the side of truth
    then I am ruthless.

If outside pressures had been effective
    our own non-violence
    would have been enough.
This condition was not fulfilled.
If the cry of guilt be raised,
    look about. Who should be blamed
    or who be praised?

Each freedom struggle
    must have its martyrs.
The Afrikaner has had his,
    now we must have ours.

    ★   ★   ★   ★

4.   Nana Sita . . .

You stand accused of refusing to move
    under the Group Areas Act.
How do you plead
    before man and his laws,
    Guilty or Not Guilty?

Guilty before man the breaker
    of hope, of home, of livelihood.
Guilty in this court of law
    but not before my Maker.

Group Areas is a wicked law,
    a degrading law, a vicious,
    humiliating and inhuman law.
As long as I live
    I shall oppose this evil.
I will not move.

Between hearth and home
    or heart of stone,
    the choice is ours.
To succumb to greed, lust, pride,
    or tread the Gandhian path, the Christian way,
    is for us to decide.
Grieve not for my shattered Third of life
    but for the treasured Whole.

Lord Krishna forgive them,
    Father forgive them
    their trespasses.

   ★   ★   ★   ★

5. Steven Biko . . .

Counsel for Biko family	*Security Police interrogators*
'Biko was found without clothes.'	'There was no room to dress him.'
'Biko was chained hand and foot to a grill for 48 hours. Would you keep a dog chained up for 48 hours? I want to know what sort of a man you are.'	'If a dog were a danger I would.'
'From where comes your power? Or are you people above the law?'	'We of the security police do not work under statute.'
'That's what we've all suspected. Thank you very much, Colonel.'	

Chant taken up after inquest verdict:

'They have killed Steve Biko. What have we done?
Our only sin is that we are black.'

      ★   ★   ★   ★

The stench of death surrounds
  a body clothed in excrement.
All the world's pain
  seems centred in his skull.
A curtain of darkness veils
  all thought, intensifying pain.
He lives in a lost world
  of nakedness and battered pride,
  of leg irons, handcuffs and jibes;
'This man is shamming.'

He takes longer to die
  than did Christ on Calvary.

Like nuclear effluent
  his pain settles on us.
Ultimately we pay the price,
  the ashes of spent lives.
Three doctors, *three*,
  observe a man's progress
  to his death, long-drawn. They arrive
  at the same comforting conclusion;
  'This man is shamming.'

Biko takes longer to die
  than Christ on Calvary.

Above the explosions of pain
  his immortal spirit roars;
'Our blackness marks us,
  it should not mock us.
'We are oppressed
  not as Zulus, Xhosas, Vendas,
  but because we are black.

'Let us accept this concept
    and turn it to our benefit.

'We must resist our fragmentation.

'Rather, let us cling tenaciously
    to each other, confounding
    the perpetrators of evil.

'While they nourish their greed
    in terms of division, of race,
    let us move as one to bestow
    upon our land a human face.'

Biko's lingering spirit takes
    longer to die than his body,
    longer than you and I.

THE DEAD

Commemorating the dead of:

Bulhoek, 1921 (163 killed)
Ngqusa Hill (near Flagstaff), 1960 (6 killed)
Sharpeville and Langa, 1960 (69 killed)
Soweto, 1976 (lowest figure of dead 292, highest estimate 750)
Sharpeville and other townships, 1984 (40 killed)
Uitenhage and other localities, mainly in Eastern Province, 1985
(A growing list of casualties)

Remembering, mourn them, for they are gone
   beyond recall. Yet grief is vain, so do not grieve
   too long. Of life, of death, which does deceive
the more, the less? A part of them lives on
   though vaguely, changeless in a changing world,
   unknown to us yet knowing us, strangely
unheedful of this our travesty
   of wasted lives, the grievous wrong that hurled
   high hopes beyond fulfilment. They are blessed,
though darkness shrouds them now, we know not where,
   it shelters them from grasp of time and care
   and grants what life withheld of peace and rest.

Make good their loss, or earth alone holds gain,
   build where the dead fall, or they fall in vain.

Imagine my misery when the history of Sharpeville was repeated at Soweto. I had known it must happen, and in feature articles to the Press had issued repeated warnings. It brings no pleasure to record this. It brings no delight to say 'I told you so.'

After Sharpeville and Langa, nothing was done to prevent a repetition. The dead were buried, the wounded went into hospital. Mr Vorster, Prime Minister at the time, denied all knowledge of any unrest in the land.

As a result of dalliance, history records Sharpeville 1960, with fear-crazed, hate-ridden policemen spewing out lethal bullets from repeater rifles, mowing down defenceless, unarmed people, young and old, male and female, carelessly, heedless of history. There followed Soweto, 1976, with heavily armed police facing children, teenagers, mowing them down, spewing out hatred, the same frenzied blood-letting, only more so, the body count being greater.

About every massacre there is a striking resemblance. It is as though the same command applies in each instance; 'The enemy is less than human, kill, kill, kill.'

When its earlier lessons go unheeded, history repeats itself. Or, say, reflections of mankind's folly appear in the guise of history revisited, for there is nothing about such recurrences to indicate the workings of a malign providence.

To all who live a normal lifespan of three score years and ten, recurring events are likely to ensue. Likewise for humanity collectively, the permutations of experience are limited, with resulting repetition. When consequences are grave, with needless suffering for many, it is wickedly foolish if no avoiding action is sought. For mankind to create one dustbowl should be enough. One massacre of non-combatants should suffice. Here is something avoidable, yet the tally mounts to our discredit: Wounded Knee, My Lai, Hill 69, Sharpeville, Wiriyamu and Chawola (Mozambique), unrecorded massacres in Guinea-Bissau, Angola, Namibia, Zimbabwe, the sly napalm incinerations in Cambodia (Kampuchea) . . . All within the lifespan of a single generation. To permit so many massacres, so many repetitions of history, warrants reproach.

For the sum of our Sharpevilles and Sowetos we carry with us our burden of shame. History has warned us, that is all it can do. We cannot vest it with human attributes or disregard its toll of suffering and sorrow. Yet it is only a matter of time, and tragedy must strike again.

From Soweto, as from Sharpeville and Viet Nam, there came a photograph to plague the vision of all who saw it; a minor repetition of history. From Sharpeville there was the photograph showing the dead and dying, the fleeing, the wounded. Over the bodies of fallen women were policemen with truncheons raised ready to club them down. From Viet Nam came the shocking photo of a napalmed child, a girl with clothing burnt away, leaving her naked. She ran screaming toward the camera as though it were her only refuge. The pain and terror registered in her eyes, her scarred body, her nakedness, must have done more to foster anti-war feelings in America than all the protest groups. From Soweto there followed the equally widely circulated evidence of man's inhumanity, a photograph showing a young student carrying the limp body of a boy, shot through the head, his face covered with blood. Alongside ran a girl in anguish, one hand raised, fingers spread wide, her face stricken with horror.

The three photographs are not the sort to grace a drawing room wall. For me they are a reminder of the solitary picture in Govan Mbeki's practically bare office. A rough cut-out from a newspaper, it was the kind to haunt one's dreams. Lumumba's pictured misery meant the dominance of power politics over peaceful transition. Govan must have seen his own frustrations mirrored in Lumumba's helplessness as death approached. Aware that his own span of life was nearing its end, he drew courage from the example of another martyr.

After the Soweto massacre it was stated that school pupils had rebelled against instruction in Afrikaans, the language of the oppressor, of limited use in a technological era. To me, this was a simplification, a glossing over of the truth. Instruction in Afrikaans is a rankling hurt because if reflects a device for keeping Africans subservient. But it does not constitute the major issue.

Searching deeper, in the Soweto riots there lay a despairing gesture, a forlorn attempt to convey the message: Our tribal

chiefs and headmen have tried, the peasants have tried; our
political leaders have tried; our elders have tried. All to no avail.
Now it is the turn of youth to rebel.

There was this further message: Our fellow blacks in
Mozambique received outside aid; Angolan blacks turned to
Cuba for help. Where can we turn, being voiceless and leader-
less? Who can hear us, who will heed us, unless we turn to
violence?

The rebellion of youth, rooted in Soweto and spreading to
other centres of discontent, stirred me to anger. It hurt to think
of so much desperation generated in the young, to find that
school children should feel the need to involve themselves in a
struggle for liberation. Where sacrifice of life is entailed it
should be those with least to lose, the middle aged and elderly,
not youngsters, who are put at risk.

Because of selfish racism, a situation has evolved in which the
young are destitute of hope. They lack real education. They
face a silicon chip future without a background of technology.
Job opportunities will be lost to them. Nothing could be more
defeating than to be forced into tribal backwardness when the
trend should be forward. Limitless scope awaits in the scientific
world of tomorrow, but not for them. Instead there is the growing threat of the Bantustans, designed to hold them back irretrievably through the conferring of alien status upon blacks
born and bred in South Africa. By depriving them of land
rights, a white ruling minority seeks to destroy all black claims
to government in "white" South Africa.

The young now realise that vague promises of a brighter
future mean nothing in the light of discredited assurances of the
past. New and brighter opportunities are wanted now, not in
some undefined tomorrow. They clamour for education befitting them for life in a world of engineering and electronics,
now, in a language suited to science, not in a pedestrian tongue
befitting the farmyard rather than the factory.

THE EXILES

Background:

* 'The young African people feel helpless. They are disillusioned. Things which seemed possible are now impossible. The easy communication races had with one another are no more. Many are turning their eyes to other lands for a better future.' (Rev. Seth Mokitimi, President, Methodist Church of S. Africa)

* Phillip Kgosana, 22-year-old Pan-Africanist leader from Cape Town, has been having a series of conferences with other exiled African and Indian congress leaders since his arrival in London from Dar-es-Salaam. He has been brought to London by the South African United Front, formed by exiled African and Indian leaders now living in London. They include Mr Nana Mahomo of the Pan-Africanist Congress, Dr Yusuf Dadoo of the Transvaal Indian Congress, Mr Oliver Tambo and leaders from S-W Africa. (News report 17th April 1961)

* 28 African political refugees flew from Francistown to Dar-es-Salaam in an airlift organised by the illegal African National Congress. A second Dakota flight – to carry another 28 Africans – will be made next week. (News report 27th Sept. 1963)

* Mr Archie Lewitton, the former hunger-strike detainee who has left South Africa, accused the Government of "manufacturing" communists to generate fear. Before leaving the country on a one-way exit permit, Mr Lewitton said: 'The South African Government is constantly finding itself short of communists. That is why they pick on every Tom, Dick and Harry. They manufacture communists, not only to impress on South Africans the so-called danger in which they live but to try to build up an image overseas as a defender of Western civilisation.' (News report 1963)

* Mr Livingstone Mqotsi, an articled clerk in a lawyer's office in Duncan Village and a man confined to the Magisterial District of East London, who had to report twice a week to the Fleet Street police station, has left the country and is believed to be in Bechuanaland. This information is contained in a tele-

gram sent by Mr Mqotsi to his wife and a friend. While members of the Special Branch were questioning his friend regarding Mr Mqotsi's whereabouts, a Post Office delivery boy arrived at the house with a telegram from Mr Mqotsi. Until the arrival of the telegram, his friend had not been able to establish Mr Mqotsi's whereabouts. Both men are banned under the Suppression of Communism Act and may not communicate with each other. (News report 30th May 1964)

* Potlako Leballo, the Pan-Africanist Congress organiser, who was once considered South Africa's public enemy number one, has flown unexpectedly out of Basutoland on a "safe conduct" pass from the South African Government. He is believed to have gone for ever. (News report 22nd Aug. 1964)

* Mr Randolph Vigne, former vice-chairman of the Liberal Party in South Africa, has asked for political asylum in Britain. It had taken him more than a month to travel a secret escape route from South Africa to Britain. (News report 15th Aug. 1964)

* Miss Selina Molteno, a 22-year-old University of Cape Town student and former international ballerina, has left Jan Smuts airport for Paris. She was held several times by Security Branch Police in Cape Town and recently went through 'four weeks of terror' which convinced her that 'the situation in this country has taken a turn for the worse.' She has arranged a job as a domestic servant in England. (News report 26th Aug. 1964)

* Mr Lionel Bernstein was given a bright and cheerful welcome by a crowd of South Africans when he arrived at London Airport last night after escaping from South Africa. (News report 3rd Sept. 1964)

* Five African children – the youngest a three-year-old – were reunited with their fugitive mothers this week after they had trekked alone through 200 miles of bush country between Johannesburg and Bechuanaland. The parents of four of the children are Mr and Mrs Duma Nokwe. Mr Nokwe, a former secretary general of the African National Congress, is at present overseas and his wife, Toni, recently left her children in Durban and escaped to Bechuanaland. The other child belongs to

Mr and Mrs Alfred Nzo. Mr Nzo is believed to be in Dar-es-Salaam. He is a former member of the ANC and at one stage held the record – 238 days for spells of 90-day detention. (News report 3rd Sept. 1964)

* Mr Pat Nakasa, the African writer who was refused a passport last week to study at Harvard University in the United States, has been given an exit permit by the Department of the Interior, which will not permit him to return to South Africa. (News report 15th Sept. 1964)

* Eusuph Ismail Omar, who arrived in London without a passport, has been granted political asylum, a British Home Office spokesman said last night. Omar, a 33-year-old shoe salesman in Johannesburg, said on his arrival last week-end that he had fled from South Africa because of daily visits by secret police. He said he had escaped from the country by walking for eight days and then hitch-hiking. (News report 16th Sept. 1964)

* Four South Africans have arrived in Dar-es-Salaam from Swaziland. They are Mr and Mrs Reg September, Dr Graham Meidlinger and Mr Oswald Dennis. All four are under banning orders in South Africa. Mr September was formerly secretary of the Coloured Peoples Congress in Cape Town. (News report 24th Sept. 1964)

* A former 90-day detainee, Mr Geoffrey Lamb – he spent 60 days in jail – has left by air for London on an exit permit. (News report 7th Nov. 1964)

* Prof. H. J. Simons, who was recently banned from further lecturing at the University of Cape Town, has left South Africa on an exit permit which prohibits him from returning. (News report 21st May 1965)

* Mr John Walmsley Blundell, chairman of Defence and Aid in the Western Cape has been served with a removal order to quit South Africa within ten days. The order adds: 'Should you fail to leave within that period the warrant for your removal will be put into operation.' (News report 9th June 1965)

* Professor Kurt Danziger, brilliant Professor of Psychology at the University of Cape Town since 1959, left South Africa

secretly on an exit permit this week. He will be unable to return. Prof. Danziger's name was in the news last year after he conducted a study into the effects of solitary confinement and took a strong stand against it. (News report 5th Aug. 1965)

* A South African Indian, Mr Abdool Karrim Essack, who was banned under the Suppression of Communism Act, has become Bechunaland's first resident attorney. Mr Essack, formerly of Maritzburg, sought political asylum after he was banned in November 1963. (News report 5th Aug. 1965)

* A Cape Town schoolteacher, Mr W. G. Alexander, M.A., of Hazendal, has left South Africa on a one-way permit, following withdrawal of his passport by the Department of the Interior. He has gone to Montreal, Canada, and his wife and eight children – including twins – will join him there later. His wife, Mrs Lilian Alexander, said: 'It broke my husband's heart to give up his South African citizenship. But when we came back to Cape Town this year, it seemed that he had been blacklisted by the Coloured Affairs Department for he was unable to get a teaching post. He was obliged to consider emigrating.' (News report 23rd Aug. 1965)

* Paul Joseph, a former executive of the Transvaal Indian Congress who was under house arrest in Johannesburg, has secretly left South Africa and is believed to be in Lobatsi, Bechuanaland. (News report 23rd Aug. 1965)

* Mr Peter Hjul, who was banned under the Suppression of Communism Act in 1963, has been granted an exit permit by the Government and will leave South Africa at the end of the month. (News report 15th Sept. 1965)

* Two weeks ago a young Transkeian, Mr Mchumano Oldjohn, left South Africa on an exit permit after being refused a passport to study on a scholarship at Lincoln University in the United States. (News report 14th Oct. 1965)

* There were moving scenes at East London Airport as a young African said goodbye to his parents, friends and country and started the first leg of his journey from South Africa on an exit permit. He is 26-year-old Lyttleton Macedisi Mngqikana, the only child of Mr and Mrs J. N. Mngqikana, of Duncan Village.

Last winter when he was offered the scholarship he applied for a passport to enable him to travel to the U.K. When he did not get a reply from the Department of the Interior, his father, who was depressed at the failure of his son to obtain suitable employment in East London and unable to attend a university because of a conviction under the Suppression of Communism Act in 1964, allowed him to apply for an exit permit. Before leaving, Mr Mngqikana said he hoped the Government would allow him to re-enter the country so that he could be of service to his people especially as there was a drain of educated Africans, most of whom have left the country. (News report 14th Oct. 1965)

* 'I am satisfied that some people have learned their lesson the hard way, especially in view of the fact that so-called leaders took the first opportunity to run away, leaving the lesser lights to hold the baby.' (Mr B. J. Vorster, Minister of Justice, later Prime Minister)

* Mr Nat Nakasa, one of South Africa's outstanding journalists, had to take an exit permit when he was refused a passport to study on a Neiman Fellowship at Harvard University in Boston last year. In June this year Mr Nakasa fell from a window on the seventh floor of an apartment building in New York. According to observers, Nakasa was 'depressed.' (News report 14th Nov. 1965)

* 'I have promised South Africa that I will act against persons who pull strings behind the scenes. I have, and nearly 900 of them have run away. You will never see them in South Africa again.' (Mr B. J. Vorster)

THE EXILES

I have seen them go
   one after another,
   to the brief joy of some
   but to my lasting sorrow.

I have felt the same despair,
   have had a stake, a share
   in their reluctance to leave
   their readiness to go.
In fitful sleep I have strayed
   down secret avenues of escape
   to the cold comfort of foreign lands
   where exiles find, among strangers,
   a ready shakedown but no warm welcome.
In search of understanding I have taken
   as my starting point their lifetime
   of unrewarded effort, of sacrifice
   penalised by prejudice.
Even so, one can but guess
   what it means to be dispossessed
   of homeland, home, and the dear
   beloved faces of yesteryear.

Listen now to names that ring familiar
   wherever freedom is a talking point,
   in the market places of the world
   and in secret where the wretched gather:

Nana Mahomo, Tennyson Makiwane, Oliver Tambo . . .

      ★   ★   ★   ★

I have watched them go
   in endless train, Africans
   leaving black Africa, reversing
   a white missionary flow.

Their departure leaves a void,
    an emptiness within, and more
    – it leaves a weakness
    in the body politic, a festering
    wound, a suppurating sore.
Our land will be the poorer
    for their going. People will plant crops
    and wonder why they wither. Building
    on shifting sands they will see
    nothing for their prosperity
    though the earth itself be rich.
When the time comes for negotiation,
    when the inevitable can be delayed
    no longer, amelioration
    like love locked out,
    may come no more, no more.
The exiles' moderating influence
    will be missed. It will be
    a hard bargain that will stem
    from less amiable men.
It seems that Government prefers to parley
    with revolutionaries rather than with men
    of less violent disposition.

Pay heed, pay tribute before too late,
    let these names reverberate
    in history's chronicle, in roll calls sounding out
    from gaps of silence, the missing and the dead:

Francis Mbelu, Gilbert Hani, Jacob Mpembe . . .

    *   *   *   *

I count their loss, and ours,
    in terms of human wretchedness,
    a house divided, a crown of thorns,
    a broken heart, a beleaguered fortress.

In the beginning, exodus
    brought silence and sadness,
    nothing more. A trickle
    does not give rise to anxiety
    but a flood presupposes doubt,
    breaches the walls of faith.
The wise will cast about,
    never too late, nor rest, nor tire,
    nor sink to hate:
    if any choice avails,
    whether to go or stay,
    we are anchored to our fate.
Above ourselves, our duty,
    beyond ourselves, our cause.
Though life be burdened with sorrow
    and hardening hardships, pause
    and repeat, 'Ungadinwa nangomso'–
                We must not tire
                        even tomorrow.

In terms of tides, of ebb and flow,
    they could not stay, they had to go.
As rivers run seaward, so our duty, sweeping on
    in torrents, now of water, now of blood. These too have gone:

Miriam Makeba, Enoch Nbhele, Nyaka Tsolo . . .

      *   *   *   *

I have watched and waited
    through many a long drear night;
    if there's a God in this fair world
    He must be on the side of might.

Meanwhile the prisons,
    our Red Hells, are filled
    to overflowing and have spilled
    into neighbouring farmlands,

creating reservoirs,
    pools of labour costing
    next to nothing.
In other parts of Africa,
    where heat is more intense than hate,
    today's black premier
    was yesterday a prisoner.
In such a climate
    martyrdom makes a man.
Here a subtle brutal strategy
    defeats martyrdom, reduces Christian charity.
Apartheid opponents are sent
    from barred cells to banishment
    without redress.
This may not represent
    fairness, justice, morality,
    but is said to be
    good politics. Good business
    too, and in Johannesburg
    financiers count their blessings
    and confer an accolade;
    'At least the Afrikaner
    is politically honest.'
In these sad days, this time
    of motives mixed with crime,
    it seems that freedom
    is nowhere to be found.

When the strain of staying grows too great,
    it is time to go. Conserving strength wisely
    we still have it. Expending it recklessly
    where is it? And where are these of late:

Moses Kotane, Robert Resha, Duma Nokwe . . .?

      ★   ★   ★   ★

I have felt the loss when they depart,
    in the marrow of my bones,
    in the strictures of my heart,
    in deep, unutterable forebodings.

I doubt if we shall see them back.
A river running wild does not return
    the rich dark silt sent down in flood.
We see through our impoverishment
    wealth gravitating to wealth,
    the enrichment of nations
    rich enough already.
Thus the Devil taunts his victims,
    maddens and makes ready to destroy,
    drives home the knife and turns it.
Look where we may, we cannot see
    an end to present suffering,
    only the sickening immortality
    of wounds too deep to heal.
This morbidity
    of thought entrances,
    makes real our purgatory.
Here at the nadir
                    we cannot sink lower.
An end has been reached, an end
    or a turning point.
Now, if we will, we can ponder anew
    the mysteries of old, then wander renewed
    where hope enhances the present
    and restores a tolerable future.

With the turning of the tide, when all is said and done,
    when rights and wrongs condense, leaving a residue
    of history, this one solid fact will hold good —
    they were not forsaking,
                    but fulfilling a mission:

Elizabeth Mafekeng, Yusuf Dadoo, Mathew Nkoana . . .

*   *   *   *

54

The forces for change are not scattered
   in weakness. They are deployed in strength.
When help comes to the needy at length,
   it springs from two sources, one near, one afar.

Personal Reflections

Through striving to appease an awesome land hunger, with fear playing upon greed, the ruling Afrikaner minority has tended to ride roughshod over others, depriving them of security. While this may ensure short term gains it is at the expense of goodwill and lasting harmony. Not only those who bear the brunt of Group Areas, the Pass Laws and Bantustans are made to feel insecure. No race, nor any individual, is immune. Although it may comfort God-fearing folk to imagine themselves ordained to take over the land, it does not follow that they must be the ones to prosper it most. Certainly it is not true of South Africa, where those who love the land sufficiently to jeopardise their future tenancy are forced into exile. Paradoxically, those who love South Africa to the extent of unmitigated self-sacrifice are the ones who must keep an ear to the ground, an eye on the door, and have their bags packed ready to go, never to return.

So it came about that in company with intimate friends I played the migratory game. In this the players look for alternative lands in which to settle if forced to leave South Africa. It is based upon the tenet that it is wise to be prepared for any emergency, while hoping that preparedness may remain a sound Scouting exercise and nothing more. It was depressing to discover that any alternative could be no better than second best. When all sentiment is removed, when all emotive overtones are dispelled, South Africa remains the first choice of all who see themselves as pioneers of a new age dawning, as well as for those who seek the good life and nothing more. Freed from the betraying fantasies of nationalism and patriotism as we were, nevertheless we found nowhere to compare with the land in which we felt so insecure.

Our version of the game went like this:

England?	Too little of the old glory remaining, too much faded splendour. In terms of population, too crowded, in terms of progressiveness, too cramped. A good country on the whole, better than many would have us believe, but we are looking for a lead, and the old country does not provide one.
Eire?	Not so crowded, not so conservative, the people hospitable but the climate unfriendly.
Channel Islands?	Standing room only during holiday seasons, no more viable than the Bantustans at other times.
Canary Islands?	Too touristic. Too many jet setters to make it appealing to visitors from a less trendy environment.
Spain?	Befitting Roy Campbell, who loved to play the swashbuckling hero. We look for a new land, yes, but not a new arena.
St Helena?	Too barren, too isolated. A prison for Napoleon. For us an escapist trap?
The Seychelles?	Too humid. Also too late. The tourists have beaten us to it.
Mexico?	Climatically suitable, but best left to the locals and retired Americans.
Canada?	Politically unsound, climatically a bleak proposition.
Australia?	Scenically flat and uninspiring, the people uncouth.
New Zealand?	The arse end of the world. Next stop the South Pole.

The process of elimination took into account most of the likely and unlikely refuges on this already overcrowded planet. Always our little games petered out inconclusively. No doubt we hoped never to play in earnest, only as a pastime.

THE INCITERS

Background:

* 'We cannot allow the republic and the future welfare of the nation to be ruined by sensation mongering, incitement or the besmirching of our country's name or that of its leaders.' (Dr Verwoerd, Oct. 1960, in radio broadcast, warning editors of English language newspapers that a politically non-conformist Press could not be tolerated).

* The march on Caledon Square police station by thousands of Africans in protest against the pass laws was recalled yesterday when 28 men, including Phillip Kgosana, 23, appeared in the Cape Town Regional Court on charges of incitement. (News report 24th Nov. 1960)

* 'At present there are more than 4,000 Africans detained in Pondoland prisons without trial, and more than 200 face charges of incitement.' (Mr Zola Sonkosi, Pondo journalist in statement from Rome, Aug. 1961)

* 'The Luthuli speeches show him up as an ordinary political inciter and agitator who envisages revolution.' (Former Minister of Foreign Affairs, Mr Eric Louw)

* 'I ask you, and all the leaders of the world, would you act differently, would you keep silent and do nothing, if you were in our place? Would you not resist if you were allowed no rights in your own country because the colour of your skin is different from that of the rulers, and if you were punished for even asking for equality?' (Miriam Makeba, South African singer)

* 'All those who think there is a possibility of a negotiated peaceful transition for sharing of power in this country are just dreaming.' (Winnie Mandela)

* 'I was motivated to fight for the freedom of my people when as a boy I listened to the elders of the tribe describing past freedom struggles under leaders such as Dingaan and Moshesh.' (Nelson Mandela, testifying at Rivonia Trial, April 1964)

* 'In the early part of April 1960 I followed in the court the proceedings when 144 young Africans were arrested in

townships around Johannesburg and charged with incitement. I listened to their long, impassioned statements concerning the grievances they regarded as intolerable, and I am bound to agree that the presiding Bantu Commissioner listened with astonishing patience. Then at the end I heard the Commissioner address the accused before giving judgement and passing sentence. In this two-hour speech all the attitudes and beliefs of authority were set out in detail. As I listened, watching the intense faces of the young, vigorous youths – many of them well educated – the thought went round and round in my mind: can tragedy take on a more Gilbertian form than this, when honest convictions can only be exchanged at a trial in court, on a statutory charge involving quite dreadful punishment?' (Rev. Arthur Blaxall)

* 'Even though the philosophers of black consciousness may be taken away, nobody can take black consciousness away from the masses.' (Dr Manus Buthelezi)

* 'Until 1976, politics was something you went into. All of a sudden, politics came to where you were – your husband was detained, your sister or brother was shot, your house was razed. A whole generation has been politicized. Black consciousness has permeated the whole of the black community. The spirit is there. To kill the spirit, you will have to kill the people.' (Bishop Manus Buthelezi)

* 'The most striking of all the impressions I have formed since I left London a month ago is of the strength of this African national consciousness. In different places it takes different forms. But it is happening everywhere. The wind of change is blowing throughout the continent.' (Mr Harold Macmillan in address to Houses of Parliament, Cape Town, 3rd Feb. 1960)

THE INCITERS

We are the spirit of protest
    heard in its first urgent form,
    the rumble of thunder
    presaging the storm.

We are the index finger pointing,
    prompting, promoting a new start,
    rather this than cleanched fist raised
    wrung from a raging heart.

We are the parent of rebellion
    husbanding its eager young,
    instilling in its offspring
    truths as yet unsung.

                    *   *   *   *

We are visionaries, seers of a sort,
    searching, seeking, sensing.
We are initiators,
    not imitators.
Oberving, we see evolution
    or in its place, revolution,
    the one aborted,
    the other thwarted,
    a situation at once corrosive,
    potentially explosive.
Otherworldly dreamers,
    impractical schemers,
    we use the burdened masses
    as our tools. Devining their needs
    we provide the spark, the animation,
    we do not make the conflagration.
We are trail blazers breaking bounds,
    braving the unknown to befriend the lost,
    preparing a path and pointing the way
    for our beleaguered brethren,
                behold the light.
We are like beacons burning bright
    beyond the barrier, the bar, the broiling sea,
    with ever a hint of danger
    a glimpse of safety.
We are bugler boys bringing
    reveille to a wearied world.

But for our rousing blasts there would be
    silence entombing the dead and the doomed,
    a perpetuation of purgatory.
We are gifted with foresight,
    but whose the power to create?
We have glimpsed a state
    fairer by far than this,
    and though we may not gain our goal
    yet we shall pursue it.
                              A fantasy?
Then you must make it real.
                              Illusory?
Then you must give it substance.
Our's the revelation, heaven sent,
    in you the promise of fulfilment.

*   *   *   *

We are idealists,
    would-be realists.
We are standard bearers marching on,
    holding high the exhortation
    to accept charge timeously,
    to rise above mediocrity.
Reaching up, we must have ideals
    by which to live, starry bright,
    always a guiding light
    advancing as we advance,
    the lure dangled before our eyes,
    urging us to move beyond
    curtains of fear, tissues of lies,
    obstructive facts, destructive myths,
    rousing us to activity though we be indolent,
    inspiring us to heroism though we be cowardly.
Higher than tempestuous seas a haven,
    above lowering skies a heaven.

Without our search for worthiness,
    life transcending worldliness,
    there would be bondage, toil to no end,
    the fusion of flesh without lifelines of love.
Our's the doctrine, your's the choice
    between incitation
                or stagnation.

★　　　★　　　✼　　　★

We are missionaries moving on,
    fishers of men casting about,
    finding enough and some left over
    for the needy, the neglected, the toilworn
    and generations as yet unborn.
We are the ferment, the yeast,
    the staff of life given purpose,
    breaking and sharing bread,
    providing more than the thin crust
    of marginal existence
    that disperses, dust unto dust.
In our calling, in our vocation,
    in our lives of dedication
    we are the thought behind the deed,
    the motive not the act,
    the stirring of a hapless nation,
    the tempter, not the temptation.
We are the spirit of renaissance
    reviving hopes long gone,
    replenishing the art of living
    which has its roots in giving.
Failing false divisions
    there is but one true way
    and that the right way. In Africa
    our's the message crystal clear, defiant,
    to rise and look about, give light
    to a late dark continent.

★　　　★　　　★　　　★

61

We are opportunists. We have not forced
   or forged an opening for ourselves.
Incitement, like the dew,
   depends upon climate;
   it does not appear by chance
   but distils, forming a heady brew
   according to circumstance.
We are like seeds awaiting
   the nod of departing winter
   the prod of approaching spring.
For all born of the flesh
   there is but one seedtime, one harvest,
   one down-to-earth reason
   to sow where seed might prosper
   in due season.
Whenever pursuit of power alone,
   or pleasure of itself,
   usurps the role of work well done
   we wait in the wings.
The moment when corruption mars the scene,
   stealing the act from honesty
   we have our part to play.
Here our cue, now to interpret
   under the spotlight, as best we may
   in costume, the comedy and the tragedy;
   from birth to death the scene is set.

★   ★   ★   ★

We appear as visionaries
   in the dark ages of mankind,
   for where is the art in living
   with hardened heart, clenched fist
                        and closed mind?

We emerge as realists
   in a world wearied of its round, an earth
   grown cold. For what is the value of struggle
   without a matching moral worth?

We arrive as missionaries
   to lead shorn flocks to pastures green.
For what is life's purpose
   if bared anxieties are all we glean?

Life is a comedy, a tragedy, a farce:
   if it becomes a shadow show and we its fallen star,
   we suggest a new direction;
   life should not descend to trivia.

We remain opportunists
   in a world of evolving chance.
For what does it profit the wealthy
   to debar the needy of change?

Personal Reflections

A phenomenon of our times is the growth of political dissent, from which arises one of our most pressing problems – what to do with dissidents.

In the case of South Africa, an outstanding example is provided by Nelson Rohinhlala Mandela, a man of national and international stature. Here are some of the bare facts in relation to him:

Born in the Transkei, 1918, of Royal blood, son of a Tembu chief.

Regardless of tribal affiliations, he gained acceptance as undisputed leader of the black liberation movement. This was a remarkable achievement for a man who lived in free association with his people for so short a time. It set him above his cousins Kaiser and George Matanzima who run the Transkeian "homeland" under the aegis of the real rulers in Pretoria, also Chief Gatsha Buthelezi of KwaZulu.

Educated Fort Hare, where he studied law. Set up legal partnership with Oliver Tambo, subsequent leader ANC in exile. Having established themselves in Johannesburg, later zoned "white", the two attorneys were forced to vacate their offices under the provisions of the Group

Areas Act. In this manner the strivings of youth were brought to nothing and the seeds of rebellion planted.

Possessing enormous appeal for the young, Nelson helped to found the Youth League of the African National Congress. From this his reputation grew. When Congress was banned, he and other high ranking officials set up *Umkhonto we Sizwe*, Spear of the Nation. Afterwards he remained on the run, gaining the sobriquet Black Pimpernel. He could have stayed abroad, but returned to face the consequences. In a despairing endeavour he wrote to the Prime Minister suggesting a national convention. His letter was disregarded. All but forgotten, in what "Pending" file does it lie today?

While Nelson Mandela was serving a 5-year sentence on a separate charge, seven of his colleagues were captured at Lilliesleaf Farm, Rivonia. Mandela, also Elias Motsoaledi and Andrew Mlangeni, charged with the seven, had their sentences extended to life imprisonment. In his concluding testimony Nelson said:

'The ANC's struggle is a truly national one. It is a struggle of the African people, inspired by their own suffering and experience. It is a struggle for the right to live. During my lifetime I have dedicated myself to this struggle of the African people. I have fought against white domination and I have fought against black domination. I have cherished the ideal of a democratic and free society in which all persons live together in harmony and with equal opportunities. It is an ideal which I hope to live for and achieve. But if needs be it is an ideal for which I am prepared to die.'

Summing up his tragic career he said:

'I followed my conscience. If I had my time over I would do the same again. So would any man who dares to call himself a man.'

In 1983, after more than 20 years on Robben Island, Mandela and others imprisoned with him were transferred to Pollsmoor Prison, Cape Town. The following year, an offer of release was made to Nelson on condition that he live in the Transkeian Bantustan. He refused this betrayal of both himself and his people. In 1985 a further offer was made to free Mandela and other ANC leaders if they agreed to renounce violence.

Nelson's response was made through his daughter Zinzie at a mass rally in Soweto. She told her audience of nearly 5,000; 'My father says he cannot and will not give any undertaking while your organisation the ANC remains banned. Your freedom and his cannot be separated. He refuses to sell the birthright of his people.'

Mandela expressed surprise at the condition set by President Botha and made five counter-demands, urging Botha (1) to renounce violence (2) promise to dismantle apartheid (3) lift the ban on the ANC (4) free political prisoners (5) guarentee free political activity.

Of all unresolved issues, the treatment of political dissidents is one that perturbs me profoundly. Because of my friendship with Govan Mbeki, one of Mandela's close associates, I am in a better position than most to see the folly of dealing with dissidents as though they are pariahs. Govan's background and Mandela's have much in common. In short, constant hounding, eventual rebellion. Mbeki shares the same fate – life imprisonment. Feeling so indebted to him for my political maturity, it grieves me to know that nothing can be done to ease his lot. As with Nelson Mandela, it was Govan's inescapable fate to become a dissident, to object to the iniquities of apartheid legislation.

Differences of opinion, whether political or otherwise, emerge from the healthy fact that no two individuals are alike. This being so, it is wrong to shatter the lives of those who hold honest convictions at variance with our own. It is opposition that keeps us on our toes, and often our supposed enemies turn out to be our greatest friends. It is self-defeating to incapacitate them.

Mass liquidation is a compounding of the same wrongful attitude and has been attempted all too often, even in recent times, as against the Palestinians. At Hitler's behest, millions of Jews and Gypsies were put to death in gas chambers. In Viet Nam the directive was given, 'Bomb them back to the Stone Ages.' Unlimited use of napalm and defoliants almost achieved this result. In Latin America, efforts have been made to wipe out all "Leftists", as though a political tag is excuse enough for their extermination. In the USSR, dissidents have been sent to

Siberia; McCarthyism was a singularly American method of dealing with dissidents. In South-West Africa (Namibia) between 1904–7, an estimated 70% of the Herero population was annihilated in an attempt at genocide. The Commander in Chief of the Colonial Force, Von Trotha, wrote; 'I believe that this nation must be destroyed as a nation.'

In South Africa, apartheid provides a breeding ground for incitation because it seeks to divide and not unify, at a time when the tendency elsewhere is toward the breakdown of racial prejudices and divisions. With dissidents so numerous, the Afrikaner ruling party has devised a wide variety of ways in which to deal with non-conformists, by means of banishment to faroff places, incarceration for life (with no remission of sentence), hanging, banning orders of differing severity, deportation, exile, one-way permits, forced removal to tribal "homelands". For long, Robben Island symbolised the ultimate in modern punitive measures.

Regardless of the methods employed, or whatever country resorts to them, it is the most deeply contemplative, caring and potentially self-sacrificing individuals who jeopardise their future wellbeing by daring to oppose a strongly entrenched, oppressive government. Uncommonly gifted with sympathy and understanding, they serve as the conscience of a nation and act as pathfinders. Imaginative, expectant of a better deal, they are capable of facing up to the challenge of change. Possessing a surplus of rare humanitarianism, they must spread it around. They see themselves as part of a whole. Idealists, they observe in society a decline, about which something must be done at street level, or governmental abuse of power will lead to an irretrievable situation. Where there is widespread disillusionment there will be dissent, and so the problem of what to do with dissidents.

In the celebrated case of Nelson Mandela, a man of royal lineage was made to wear sackcloth while his lowly bred warders strutted round bedecked in uniforms complete with braid. The result was deep embitterment, rising and reaching out to others. This is what *not* to do with political dissidents. Then what to do with them? They should be accorded the status and rights of prisoners of war.

I am reminded of the case of ten Puerto Rican guerillas

charged with conspiring to overthrow the US Government. Comprising six men and four women, they appeared in a Chicargo court handcuffed and shackled with leg irons. In defiance they shouted 'We are prisoners of war'.

A further news report of recent times has a pathetic ring. It states: 'South Africa's police are running short of leg irons, and have advertised for 200 extra pairs. Many prisoners are routinely put in leg irons to prevent violence and escape, according to evidence given at last year's inquest on Steve Biko, the black leader who died in police custody.'

THE DETAINEES

Background:

* Looksmart Solwandle Ngudle, a 90-day detainee, was found dead, hanging by the neck from his belt in a police cell at Pretoria North police station last week, the Commissioner of Police, General J. M. Keevy, said in Pretoria yesterday. (News report 26th Sept. 1963)

* Mr Berrange, Q.C., for Ngudle's widow and relatives:

Adjutant Officer J. C. E. Earle, S. A. Police:

'Is it correct to say that Ngudle just had to lie or sit in his cell for 23 hours, day after day after day?'

'Yes.'

(News report 28th Nov. 1963)

* The case of an Indian, Ebrahim Sinyanvala, has shocked the country. He was detained last June and later released. On his way home he was detained again for a traffic offence. He ran away, and two days later his body was found in a river near the police station. He had preferred suicide to facing a return to the police cells. (News report from England, 13th Oct. 1963)

* Concern about the treatment of South African political detainees held under the "90-day law" without being brought to trial has been reinforced by the haggard appearance of eleven political leaders of all races who appeared in the Pretoria courts last week charged with planning to overthrow the Government. Their counsel successfully argued that they were in no condition to stand trial. . . . Detainees now released describe the mental torture as almost unbearable. (News report 13th Oct. 1963)

* Two Cape Town 90-day detainees, Mr T. Tsotso and Mr N. Maingizane, are under observation in Valkenberg Mental Hospital after being committed there on the advice of two doctors and through a magistrate in terms of the law. (News report 19th Nov. 1963)

* The Minister of Justice, Mr Vorster, said last night that he was fully aware that certain 90-day detainees had been examined by psychiatrists. (News report 18th Nov. 1963)

* Isaac Tlale said he was arrested in August last year, in Alexandra Township and kept in solitary confinement. He was never allowed out of his cell, even for exercise. (News report 28th Nov. 1963)

* Mrs Suzman maintained that it was wrong to call the Act the 90-Day Act. The Minister could hold people at his pleasure indefinitely. Some were serving a third 90-day period. (House of Assembly, 22nd Jan. 1964)

* Commenting on the general question of the 90-day law, Mr Vorster said the Act was clear: it provided for terms fo 90 days. He did not think it was unfair to hold a man for further terms of 90 days, assuming the circumstances justified this. Asked how long a 90-day man could be held, he said it depended on the circumstances. If, for instance, he would not give information to the police, the authorities had no option but to detain him longer. (Interview with Mr B. J. Vorster, 1964)

* A hushed House of Assembly yesterday heard Mrs Helen Suzman quote statements made by 90-day detainees alleging ill-treatment through being beaten with batons, kicked and pushed, having their heads covered with plastic hoods, and being given electric shocks. Mrs Suzman also referred to 'the filthy conditions of the toilets, the lack of blankets and the shocking food.' If assaults were reported to the chief wardens it resulted in detainees being beaten up by the wardens. (News report 23rd Jan. 1964)

* 'In 1963 there were 17 cases of policemen assaulting witnesses in criminal trials and 44 assaults by the police on prisoners.' (Mr Hamilton Russell)

* Next of kin have not "in every case" been advised. The wife of one detainee did not know he had died till after his burial, and women have waited for months for news of even the whereabouts of their incarcerated husbands and sons. Nor is this all. The families of many innocent people, discharged after long periods without even being brought to trial and in some cases

not even interrogated, have been made to suffer much privation. Furthermore the victim himself often lost his job and later was "endorsed out" of the area where he worked. (*Evening Post* leader 17th June, 1964)

* Mr Berrange said observers had found that after one to three days prisoners in solitary confinement showed signs of bewilderment, discouragement at attempts to fraternise; after between three and ten days confinement prisoners showed signs of gradual compliance and between ten days and three weeks a tendency to automatic behaviour. Later, detainees experienced hallucinations and had difficulty in distinguishing between truth and fiction. After months of detention they were depressed, frequently to the point of suicide. (Mr V. C. Berrange, Q.C.)

* 'The mental torture consisted of confinement alone within four grey walls with nothing to do, no one to speak to and nothing to read. Although I disliked talking to policemen I had found interrogation by the police a distinct relief.' (Evidence of Lionel Bernstein, one of Rivonia Trial accused)

90-DAY DETENTION ABOLISHED . . . .

* *January 11th, 1965:* Twenty months ago today, Security Police swooped on homes throughout South Africa and arrested 14 people – the first 90-day detainees.

The General Law Amendment Act had become law only ten days before the swoop, in a 30-word announcement in the Government Gazette Extraordinary. Today, the last 73 of South Africa's detainees will be freed or charged, and the most controversial clause in the Act will be suspended.

During the twenty months in which 90-day detention has been in operation, more than 950 people have been detained, about 500 charged and the rest released without charge.

. . . . *180-DAY DETENTION INTRODUCED*

* *The Agony Increases:* By constantly being subjected to stronger and stronger doses of undemocratic law and authoritarian action, people become used to it and accept it as normal.

Under this process 90-days becomes extended to 180-days. (*Cape Times* leader)

* Mystery surrounded the whereabouts of South Africa's first 180-day detainee, Mr Isaac Heymann, late last night – hours after the Supreme Court had ruled his "detention" unlawful and ordered his discharge. Banned under the Suppression of Communism Act in September 1961, Mr Heymann was also one of the last people to be held under the 90-day law – 11 days before the clause was suspended in January. (News report 10th Sept. 1965)

* After two Supreme Court hearings and a flurry of action by lawyers the Government, Security Police and his wife, 45-year-old Isaac Heymann was last night still South Africa's only 180-day detainee. (News report 11th Sept. 1965)

* Nine days after Mr Heymann's detention his wife, Mrs Anne Heymann, brought an urgent application to court for his release. The order for his release was granted on the grounds that the Minister of Justice had failed to frame the regulations governing detention. Mr Heymann was immediately arrested on a charge under another Act. The following morning his wife brought a Habeas Corpus application to court which ordered that he be produced before 2 p.m. that day. At 1.27 p.m. the regulations controlling the detention of people under the 180-day clause were promulgated and Mr Heymann was immediately re-detained. He was not produced in court. (Subsequent news report)

* The conduct of the Security Police in the case of Mr Isaac Heymann, South Africa's first 180-day detainee, has done the country a disservice and merited the censure of the court, Mr Justice Bresler said in the Supreme Court, Pretoria. (News report 14th Sept. 1965)

* The arbitrary manner in which the Special Branch arrested Mr Heymann as a witness under the 180-day clause, then released him only in order to rearrest him immediately under the Suppression of Communism Act, and finally again detained him as a witness constituted a demonstrable abuse of the powers vested in the Minister of Justice by Parliament. (*Eastern Province Herald* sub-leader)

DETAINEE
90-DAYS . . . . . .

180-DAYS . . . . . .

Grey walls grey, grimly grey,
    grey forbidding walls, gravely grey,
    grey pallor of skin deprived of sunlight,
    grey like the captive walls,
    grey like a mud-caked hippo's hide,
    grey like a Queen ant buried within
    the King's dark chamber.
Ceiling beyond reach, grey beyond belief,
    ceiling beyond touch, entombing grief,
    high ceiling providing protection,
    lending distance in the wrong direction.
High dome with not a single rafter,
    veiling Venus, masking Mars,
    nudging out the day, the night,
    dispensing nothingness as a human right,
    dispersing the prayer for life hereafter;
    this one life is enough.
Barred window, pittance in a world of plenty,
    hinting at freedom while withholding it,
    single window set in the south wall
    away from the westering sun,
    high window hiding the sun, the moon,
    where the long shadows of late afternoon?
Window on my world, ridiculously barred, so high,
    window beyond reach, life passing me by.

This the domicile
                for solitude.

*   *   *   *

One mattress shared with innumerable lice,
    one worn blanket with accompanying fleas,
    one makeshift pillow, a bucket lavatory.

72

This the inventory
            of despair.

    ★   ★   ★   ★

Where to turn from pacing, where next,
    north or east? How not to be perplexed
    by south, by west? The sun rises, but where,
    where does the sun rise? And where is west,
    where the home for moon, for sun,
    once the daily round is done?
One sterile day passes, and another,
    calendar days stalking each other,
    solemn procession of skeletal days,
    a following train of ghostly nights.
Within four walls freedom has a hollow ring,
    is there any such thing?
The walls are here,
    but freedom, where?
Small world of sullen silence
    lending itself to pretence,
    self-held conversations,
    earnest deliberations
    on this and that triviality,
    supposing oneself to be
    the other. What other?
                    Either there is God
    or no God.
Wish I could break the silence with sound
    of crashing crockery.
And oh! to hear the milkman's clattering round.

Not to think, not to think.
In this drear world to keep tight rein
    on thought, hold in check
    the plunging future and the rearing past,
    stay the vision's darting dancing speck
    of hope, and there remain fast.

Think of evil, think no good, be perverse,
    dull the intellect, stifle thought,
    schooling in reverse.
Breach the walls of faith, mar the memory,
    mask out love, religion set to nought.
In a senseless sexless void set free
    all thoughts of madness nor leave
    a gap for it to fill.
Let thoughts take wing
    to soar above this dark and brooding ill.
Now think of birdsong
                or think of nothing.

What fools men are. Fools and knaves
    to ensnare the lives of others,
    turning freemen into slaves
    though all are brothers.
Fools to think they can imprison
    without being imprisoned, brutalize
    without being brutalized.
What fools they.
                Here comes one
    bringing slops, the same unsavoury fare
    grudgingly prepared, cooked without care,
    served with ill grace.
                Waiter, waiter,
    warder, warder speak by choice,
    free of interrogation, one word
    that echos not your master's voice.
Speak for once without profanity,
    say something for my hearing's sake
    and for the sake of sanity.
So . . . you pass the plate
                without a word,
    a whisper might be overheard.
Four courses served as one
    and duty's done.
Waiter, where the condiments, the sauces?

Where are they now, friends of the past,
   friends and lovers, young and old?
Is there nothing love can outlast?
How firm is friendship, how loose its hold?
And what of loneliness that extends
   beyond grey walls to ageing friends?

Father, father, at your side
   I brushed away unmanly tears – remember?
Yet, last night – all night – I cried.
Mother, mother, on your fond knee
   I heard tell of God, but where
   in this grey world is He?
Father, mother, wait for me,
   your son's homecoming depends
   upon silence or its breakdown, it extends
   in multiples of ninety,
   the ratio of man's inhumanity.
Dear Lord! here there is need of muscle, more
   than is hinged in flesh and bone,
   or required to pull on oars
   and excavate from solid stone.

When to hear voices other than my own
   and my inquisitors?
When an act of kindness shown
   by my tormentors?
Oh to hear inconsequential chatter
   in place of oaths and blasphemies,
   words weather-wise and warm,
   charged with superficial laughter,
   talk of things that do not matter,
   pearls of wisdom lingering after
   the spread of rumours, banalities, trivialities.
Voices raised but not demanding, insistent or obscene,
   words seldom subtle and never mean,
   unlike my torturers' 'Tell, tell
   or we'll give you a taste of hell.'

Speak of the devil! Here he comes
    flanked by fallen angel Van,
    another of the subspecies,
    ape dressed up as man.

'Come, my friend, be reasonable, for we
    are reasonable men.
We don't want to hurt you,
    do we Van? But we have our duty
    and we are dutiful men, eh Van?
Speak and you can go tomorrow, free
    and with money in your pocket.
For we are reasonable men. Only tell
    or we'll turn life into ruddy hell.
Now you mute swine tell, spill the beans
    or we'll set to use our means
    of gentle persuasion, eh Van?
Come you bastard tell, tell
    or we'll strip you naked
            shake you
            shock you
            break you
    but we'll make you tell. Van
    this is going to be hilarious, a farse.
Connect the electric shocker, set it up
    for fifty volts, one lead on his penis
    the other up his arse.
But we won't mark him, not a graze.
We'll give him one more chance
    and failing that, another ninety days.'

Four grey walls and ashen skin
    with mystery locked within:
    Save yourself,
                    don't sell yourself.
This the only mastery
    of self and others.
Here in this solumn cell
    the power that calls for courage,
    not to tell.

Here within four walls the irony
    of mastery,
                    the key to power
    that lies in mystery.
Bravery for the sake of mystery,
    mystery for the sake of mastery.
The secret locked within forever,
    an act of non-betrayal, not to tell,
    not as a last resort,
    no, never, never.

Where the greater heroism to be found,
    on playing field, on battle ground
    or in cells of solitude, with no applause,
    no show of bravery, no pretence,
    lacking an audience?
Where the path for kindred nations
    from Genesis through to Revelations?
Do we, as wardens of mankind
    seek justice or success?
Do we, as warders on our rounds
    progress or retrogress
    from prison cell to torture chamber?
Are we, as wardens of the future
    on our way up
    or on our way out?

Is it the thought of yesterday that haunts
    or the fear of tomorrow that taunts?
Not so much the question of origin
    as of destiny that daunts?

The crucial test since time began
    the entombing of humanity,
    the denouncement of human rights,
    the triumph of science, the defeat of man.

THE ARENA

Background:

* 'When a man commits a crime for which he is charged, convicted and sentenced, then dies in custody for any reason other
than neglect, torture or murder, no blame attaches to officials of
the State. But when a man is detained without trial, then dies a
violent death in captivity, his captors are automatically to blame
for his death. Therefore we accuse the captors of Mapetla
Mohapi of being responsible for his death. Theirs is the guilt,
and it is shared by every person in this country who supports
the atrocity of detention without trial.' (*The Times*, England)

* 'He (Mapetla Mohapi) was a man of great inner resources,
confident and committed to his cause.' (Father Stubbs, Community of the Resurrection)

* One of Mapetla Mohapi's working colleagues:
'He was a driving force behind us and a true fighter. During
times of difficulty he was the one who kept us going and strong.
His analysis of detention was that it was important in the
struggle to survive all the blows meted out by the system.'

* 'Now you see how Mapetla died.' (Captain Hansen to Miss
Thenjiwe Ntintso, while she was undergoing torture)

* 'Mapetla welcomes you.' (Words spoken by jailor displaying
doll hanging by neck)

* The Mohapi "suicide note" was definitely written with a
different pen from that used for three letters the detainee wrote
before his death, a police handwriting expert told the Grahamstown Supreme Court yesterday.
Lieutenant-Colonel Frederick Fourie said he had no doubt a
different pen had been used, since the ink on the suicide note
was considerably darker than that on the three toilet paper
letters.
He was giving evidence for the third consecutive day in the
civil action Mrs Nohle Mohapi brought over the death of her
husband, Black Consciousness leader, Mr Mapetla Mohapi, in
August 1976. Mrs Mohapi is suing for $35,000. She claims her

husband did not hang himself as alleged by the State but died as a result of assaults by his Security Police interrogators.

The suicide note found on his clothing the next day is a forgery, she alleges. (*Eastern Province Herald*, 1st March, 1980)

* Demands for a full inquiry into the treatment of detainees have increased in a storm of anger over the death of Steve Biko, the 19th black to have died in detention over the past 18 months.

Justice Minister Jimmy Kruger announced yesterday that Mr Biko, 30, one of South Africa's foremost black activists and an ardent proponent of the Black Consciousness movement, died on Monday night after a seven-day hunger strike.

His death brought to 19 the number of blacks who have died in the past 18 months while detained under security laws which allow indefinite detention without trial. Other deaths have been officially attributed to suicide by hanging or jumps and falls from buildings.

Dr Nthato Motlana, a leading figure in the nearby black township of Soweto, said he was disturbed by the growing number of people, apparently in good health, who died in detention. (News report, Johannesburg, 14th Sept. 1977)

* Three South African newspapers have carried reports that Steve Biko did not die from hunger strike. One of those papers, *The World*, has now been banned by the authorities. The *Rand Daily Mail* was taken to the South African Press Council by Mr Kruger after a front page story claiming that Steve Biko had suffered extensive brain damage. The Johannesburg *Sunday Express* said that sources connected with the forensic investigation said brain damage had been the cause of death.

Steve Biko was arrested on August 18, 1977. He was taken to Port Elizabeth and on September 11 moved 700 miles to Pretoria, where he died on September 12. He was 30 years old and said by relatives to have been extremely fit when arrested. (News report following Biko's death)

* Asked today if the medical evidence was compatible with self-inflicted wounds, Mr Kruger (Minister of Justice) said; 'I do not know if they were self-inflicted, but I often think of banging my own head against a wall.' (News report 9th Nov. 1977)

* 'Frankly I would prefer Mr Biko to be alive.' (Justice Minister Kruger, Pretoria, 9th Nov. 1977)

* Mr Biko died on September 12 from head injuries. These probably had been sustained during an interrogation room scuffle with security police on September 7. (Magistrate's finding, Biko inquest)

* From address by counsel for Biko family, Mr Sydney Kentridge, at Biko inquest:
'Upon being called in, Dr Ivor Lang gave a patently false certificate. Neither he nor his superior, Dr Benjamin Tucker, made any inquiry of their patient as to the origin of even the lip injury which, at least, they admit seeing. They did not even direct any inquiry to the police. This studied lack of curiosity can only be explained by their active collaboration with the police or a deliberate election not to embarrass the police, nor indeed themselves, by asking questions to which the answers were obvious. . . . The police felt confident they could rely upon the doctors to support them, and their confidence was justified. Perhaps strengthened thereby they, with gross impertinence, presented to this court a totally unplausible account of Mr Biko's death, starting with a fanciful description of a struggle violent in the extreme in which no blow was struck, a bizarre account of an alleged shamming when to any candid observers a man's progress to his death was being seen . . .'

* Mr P. R. van Rooyen, SC, for the police, asked Dr Lang; 'I suppose you have been lying awake at nights, worrying, since Mr Biko's death?' Dr Ivor Lang; 'Very many nights.' (News report on inquest)

* 'I believe the truth will come out.' (Mr Biko's wife, Ntsiki)

* 'I am extremely distressed to hear of the death of Steve. I admired him greatly. The price that will have to be paid by this country for his death under these circumstances will be very high.' (Chief Gatsha Buthelezi)

* 'Only a country as mad as South Africa can waste such talent.' (Chief Gatsha Buthelezi)

* 'They asked me if I knew Looksmart Ngudle. I was told he was detained under the 90-Day law and he died in his cell. I was told that if I did not tell them what they wanted I would also die in my cell. Even my own people would not know what had happened to me.' (Nicolaas Mapipa, 35, in Regional Court, Cape Town, who alleged he was threatened while being held under 90-Day detention clause)

* Looksmart Ngudle, died September 5, 1963. Inquest verdict: 'Suicide, hanging.' (News report)

* Nicodimus Kgoathe, died February 5, 1969. Post-mortem showed broncho-pneumonia, possibly as a result of head injuries. Had bruises and abrasions from having 'slipped in shower.' Doctor believed these injuries were due to assault. Inquest magistrate said that on evidence before him he was unable to record a finding. (News report)

* James Lenkoe, died March 10, 1969, Pretoria prison. Traces of copper, signs of electric shock in toe; bruises below ear, marks on neck, shoulders; haemorrhage at base of skull. Magistrate found 'suicide by hanging', death not due to offence on part of anyone. (News report)

* Mr B. J. Vorster, Minister of Justice, said in an interview that he had called for a full report on the case of three-times detained Elijah Loza of Cape Town. At the same time, Mr Vorster said that a third term of 90 days could well be justified in principle. (News report, 7th Nov. 1963)

* Imam Abdullah Haron, died Sept. 27, 1969 in Maitland, Cape, police cells. 'Fell downstairs'. Had 26 bruises of different ages, broken rib, haematoma on back. Inquest magistrate unable to determine how balance of injuries sustained. 'Detainee died of heart trouble partly brought on by injuries.'

* Solomon Modipane, died Feb. 28, 1969. 'Slipped on soap in shower.' District surgeon unable to determine cause of death. Magistrate endorsed documents 'natural death – no inquest necessary.'

* Suliman Saloojee, died Sept. 9, 1963. 'Death from multiple injuries. No irregularities.'

* Mr Saloojee, who had been under detention for 65 days, threw himself from the seventh floor window of The Greys, the police headquarters in Johannesburg, yesterday. A 14-year-old schoolboy of Fairview said he saw a tall Indian standing at a seventh floor window of the police building. A moment later he jumped and soon afterwards three heads appeared at the window of the room. The Chief of the Special Branch Police, Brigadier H. J. van den Bergh, confirmed that Mr Saloojee jumped to his death, and at the time he was under interrogation. (News report, 10th Sept. 1964)

* General Hendrik van den Bergh, former head of the powerful Bureau for State Security (BOSS) at Erasmus Commission, investigating Information Department scandal involving Dr Cornelius Mulder, Dr Eschel Rhoodie, Mr B. J. Vorster, Gen. v.d. Bergh and others:
'Mister Commissioner, I want to tell you truly that with my department I can do the impossible . . . I can tell you today, not for your records, but I can tell you I have enough men to commit murder if I say to them "Kill".'
Judge Erasmus: 'Yes?'
Van den Bergh: 'I don't mind who the victim is. That is the type of men I have. Afrikaners. I have good men.' (News report, 16th May, 1980)

THE ARENA

Recalling a few of those who failed
to beat the count, who did not survive
the brutalities of interrogation.

Seconds out:

In an aside, a spectator proclaims;
    'Biko's death leaves me cold.'
It is the Minister of Justice, no one less,
    speaking from his ringside seat,
    elegantly attired in evening dress,
    his Dutch courage making bold;
'Biko's death leaves me cold.'

The Fight is on:
>Though battered, bewildered,
>>we are not yet beaten.
>As lightweights tackling heavies
>>we battle against the odds. A hard bout
>>is at hand. Outweighed, the contest levies
>>its toll. We dare not stand
>>>>and slug it out.
>We spar for openings,
>>duck and dodge,
>>smother and spoil,
>>mar and maul.
>Life is a bruising encounter
>>for the handicapped, the poor.
>We jolt and jar to score,
>>to survive we weave and wave
>>but do not wilt.

>Beyond the barriers of pain
>>there appears a vision,
>>a sturdy chain
>>of champions of the past:

Looksmart Ngudle
>>Mapetla Mohapi
>>>>Steven Biko . . .

The Crowd Roars:
>Above the clamour of the crowd,
>>echoing, a jailor's jibe
>>>>is heard:
>'This is how Mapetla died.'

>The blows that breach our worn defence
>>are blows that beat a swift tattoo
>>of solid leather pounding flesh;
>They rain on all, on us, on you.
>The torture chamber's throngs enthuse;
>>'Observe how long it takes,
>>how much the body can endure

83

before it breaks!'
The tired brain dispels the thought;
    'If this be all of life,
    to wish away its minutes
    and achieve a moment's rest.'

Between the rounds a second seeks
    to lend support. He speaks
    to subdued spirit; 'Remember floored battlers
    rising from defeat:

Nicodimus Kgoathe
        James Lenkoe
            Elijah Loza . . .'

The Fighting Heart:
        Far from the ring, in Biko's cell appears
        a jailor with a dangling doll
        hanging by its neck.
    'Mapetla welcomes you', the jailor jeers.

    The poor and the brave have this in common;
        they are lonesome.
    But the one submits, the other fights on.
    We must not suffer lasting defeat.
    Between indifference and death
        there is a slender margin.
    With each round the ring becomes
        a diminishing world. We lean
        against the ropes for support.
    We must fight on. We must not be seen
        to falter. Between defeat and death
        there is little to choose.
    Both are losses. We give of our all.
    To fend off wretchedness we need
        heroes at our beck and call,
        we are not sufficient unto ourselves.
    If we stand alone we fall,
        we need a pillar of support.

In our corner never failing,
    we look for martyrs, brave souls who have fought
    and overcome, symbolizing victory
    snatched from defeat.

In answer to our call they come
    like phantom fighters,
                    golden gloved,
    wearing the belt of martyrdom:

Imam Abdullah Haron
            Solomon Modipane
                        Suliman Saloojee . . .

THE AGITATORS

Background:

* 'Every Afrikaner and every white man is today bartered for the price of a cheap agitator.' (Dominee G. J. J. Boshoff, political predikant of Linden, Johannesburg, 1960)

* 'There has been systematic propaganda against the Bantu Authorities Act and agitators have taken full advantage of this.' (Mr M. D. C. de Wet Nel, Minister of Bantu Administration and Development, speaking in House of Assembly, 1960)

* 'We have had trouble in Sekhukuniland, Zeerust and now Pondoland. One thread running through these troubles is resistance to the Bantu Authorities system, and the Government simply cannot blink the fact and put it all down to agitators.' (Mr Quintin Whyte, Director of South African Institute of Race Relations, 1960)

* Measures to control the movements of agitators into and out of Pondoland, including the establishment of a home guard under the Bantu Authorities with powers to apprehend intruders, including whites, and hand them over to the police, were announced by the Minister of Bantu Administration and Development, Mr de Wet Nel, at a Press conference in Pretoria. (News report 23rd Nov. 1960)

* 'Agitators, activated by foreign doctrines, instigated tribesmen against what they called tribalism and painted vivid pictures of a multi-racial Utopia in South Africa.' (Mr J. H. Abraham, Commissioner-General for Xhosa National Unit, 1960)

* 'As far as it is in our ability we will keep the country as secure as it is, because we are not prepared to allow our lives, properties and security to be endangered by a small number of agitators.' (Mr B. J. Vorster, Johannesburg, Nov. 1964)

* 'Another threat to South Africa comes from people who are not necessarily communists. Parliament has charged me to determine whether these people are a danger to the country. These are the people who agitate for one man one vote. I will not hesitate to take action against them.' (Mr B. J. Vorster, 1964)

* 'The time has come for the whole of humanity to shout halt and to act with firmness to stop these crazy rulers from dragging our country into a horrifying disaster.' (Miriam Makeba, African singer testifying at her own request before United Nations special committee on apartheid, July 1963)

* 'I can't help feeling that political agitation is increasing throughout the world and those from whom it emanates are becoming stronger.' (Mr Reginald Honey, S.A. representative, International Olympic Committee, Oct. 1965)

* 'We shall fight them on the beaches, we shall fight them on landing grounds, we shall fight them in the streets and in the hills. We shall never surrender.' (Winston Churchill, in speech after Dunkirk)

* 'Those who profess to favour freedom, and yet deprecate agitation, are men who want crops without plowing up the ground. They want the ocean without the awful roar of its waters.' (Frederick Douglass)

* 'Agitators do not themselves create grievances. They use available facts to exploit a situation.' (Credo Mutwa, Soweto herbalist, 1980)

* 'We were labelled political agitators, which I certainly am not.' (Mr Qeqe, Soweto, detained by Security Police after 60 days without being charged)

* 'Whatever may or may not be the contribution of "enemies of South Africa" from outside to the situation and however much intimidation plays a part, the present unrest cannot be dismissed as simply "the work of agitators"' (Rt Rev Kenneth Oram, Anglican Bishop of Grahamstown, July 1980)

THE AGITATORS

In the beginning was the WORD
    cleaving silence,
    simple deed of dedication
    cutting through the void,
    initial act of agitation.

87

We, the agitators,
   are revivalists, re-creators.
Ours the calls, the thunderings
   for further sunderings
   of silence,
   lest silence should reign
   and living lapse again.
Through agitation, from promotion
   of responsible commotion,
   comes change, comes chance.
Let there be chance
               let there be change:
   this, the first law of life.
In our origin
   there is no mystery,
   only readings and mis-readings
   of history.
Repression, the dearth
   of chance, of change,
   of self-expression, gives birth
   to agitation.
In a world of neglect, of war and want,
   we are the shock troops moving ahead,
   the night watch and the dawn patrol
   on guard against decline.
We are the cavalry
   moving into line,
   the chargers, the breakers,
   the progress makers.
Ere the battle takes its toll,
   prior to calling of the roll,
   the few must be heard
   to agitate. Agitate
   or abdicate.
In answer to the call
   the many must be seen to stand,
   stand and be counted,
   stand or fall.
Before too late,
   the will to agitate

or surrender all
to the all-powerful State.
When government, entrenched in power,
usurps rights and dispenses favour,
our bounden duty is to see
that their 'forever'
is less than eternity.
In last resort, as agitators
we are funeral directors,
undertakers of timeworn tradition,
of narrow nationalism.

Where tyranny and cant abound,
where colour, race and creed are issues
of devisiveness, there we may be found
pointing, probing, paring tissues
beneath the crust, the meagre skin
that lies but wafer thin.
PASS LAWS, like war games, exist
to be abolished,
and we can win if we persist.
Where TOWNSHIP, COMPOUND, LOCATION,
are other words for ghettos
hedging people in,
they stand to be demolished:
come, let us begin
with agitation.
Where INFLUX CONTROL curtails
movement for the many,
it restricts an entire nation
leaving, when all else fails,
nothing save agitation.
Why wait to be ENDORSED OUT?
Rather a whimper, better a shout
than tame submission.
The insecure foundation
of GROUP AREAS
necessitates the nudge
of agitation.

BANTU AUTHORITIES, high-sounding edifice,
   is a rampart to be laid low,
   but only by blow on blow.
All are impoverished
                  by RACE CLASSIFICATION,
   for all belong, demonstrably
   through agitation,
   to life's rich diversity.
WHITE PRIVILEGE may be the rule, the rock,
   the pillar, law of the land, momentarily,
   but what of future shock,
   and what of divinity?
Pride may extend
   to SEPARATE ENTRANCES,
   but to what end
   when all leave by the same exit?
From ACADEMIC SEGREGATION
   we learn a vital lesson,
   the need for agitation.
Much as nature may abhor
   a vacuum, and its dissipation,
   so to us the IMMORALITY ACT
   constitutes bad law
   and leads to agitation.
The strands of race are running out
   for BEACH APARTHEID,
   come high tide and turn about.
Last but not least,
   JOB RESERVATION,
   once a raging beast,
   tamed of necessity and by virtue of
                  agitation.

★   ★   ★   ★

Nature, never dormant, agitates
   for good reason, quietly
   as a rule, sometimes violently,

and ever without fear or favour.
It changes seasons fairly,
    not for privilege,
    rotates its crops
    without seeming to do so.
    Nature, indifferent to success,
    agitates for change.

Whipped by wind and wave
    the oceans are troubled none the less
    by stealth, by stillness,
    by tidal scourings left undone,
    by spindrift and pollution.

The earth, ever restive,
    tilts and turns to good effect,
    evolving days and nights,
    providing interrelation
    by way of dawns and dusks,
    forever changing station
    within the ambit of impartial law.
Moon and sun deflect its oceans,
    push and pull of time and tide
    promoting life through agitation.
The earth, seeming static
    while the stars race round,
    agitates for change,
    the law we cannot rearrange,
    the wheel to which all are bound.

Agitate, agitate,
    and the wheel revolves.
Agitate, agitate,
    and life, in truth, evolves.
Agitate, before too late
    agitate for freedom
    and freedom come.

For 13 years I worked for a highly respected firm of motor assemblers and distributors in Uitenhage, Eastern Province of South Africa. The elderly Production Manager was a character of a kind seldom encountered nowadays. He had been with the firm from its inception, and knew every item of equipment, every make and model that had rolled off the final assembly line. He had undergone no technical training, but having lived with motor cars all his working life he knew every nut and bolt that went into their construction. Holding a responsible post at a late stage in life, it was not surprising that he could be rather crotchety, though full of fun when at his amiable best. Though often grumpy when approached about problems of production, there were times when he enjoyed ragging me. His favourite ruse was to ferret in a bottom drawer of his desk and produce a candle mounted in a holder from a bygone age, round the base of which was inscribed the words *QUO VADIS?*

Shaking with mirth while presenting it to me, he would look from face to face of the essential audience to see what effect his little joke was having. Paunchy and heavily built, he gave vent to belly laughs which shook his entire frame.

'*Quo Vadis?*' he would roar, '*Quo Vadis*, Earl?'

I may have made a slip in the planning of production, though as a rule my work was accurate. It mattered not. As his junior I served as a target for his wit.

The old man was a character in his own right, though I may not have remembered him through the years had it not been for his candlestick, with its questing *QUO VADIS?* Because of it, I recall his pantomime act from time to time, with its theatrical gestures and accompanying belly laughs. Then a query of my own arises. Did he have a foreboding of my expulsion from South Africa? Did he know of my exile to come? Certainly it was not the quality of my work that he was questioning. So why his favourite joke with its probing sentiment, reserved for me? To my knowledge his candlestick was not proffered to anyone else in all the years I knew him. He held me in high esteem and was aware of my political writings, which appeared frequently in local newspapers. Then was he seeking to forestall tragedy, of which he had a presentiment? Aware of imminent danger, knowing me to be too stubborn for coercion, was he seeking to light the way with his candle and show of good humour?

Another episode from my working days in Uitenhage, with a similar underlying element of grief, springs to mind.

Early in my association with the firm I gained a vicarious delight from walking the length of the chassis assembly line. There, looking so much a part of the scene as to be indispensable, was a burly Xhosa with bulging biceps and barrel chest. No misfit he. Whether wielding hammer or wrench, his massive shoulders took the strain. His particular part in the assembly procedure called for no little skill and a great deal of physical strength. He possessed the one in adequate measure, while of the other he had an abundance. He reminded me strongly of Paul Robeson in his chain gang role, with the difference that he was a worker in a real life situation, not an actor with a make believe part to play.

It was a factual situation in more than one respect. He was performing a task for which he was as suited as the fabled village smith; in addition he was breaking the colour bar. His was the only non-white face on the assembly lines at that time. More to the point, he was the only non-Afrikaner.

Some Xhosas are surprisingly fair skinned, others are dark. This amiable fellow was black, coal black, pitch black, black-black. He was intelligent by any standard, and from all points of view it pleased me to see him there. Everything about him proclaimed his rightness to be on the job.

Except that he was black. Black-black. As black as any man could be. For this reason he was transgressing the industrial colour bar, known as Job Reservation. So was the firm for employing him, a black man in a position reserved for whites.

While deriving pleasure from his presence, I experienced also a deepening sense of unease springing from the knowledge that the spell could be broken, whereupon my extraneous thrill and the man's sense of pride in his work, so obviously displayed, would be brought to nothing.

Even then, covetous eyes were being cast in his direction and rumblings of discontent were mounting. Murmurs of protest from the white trade union: 'This is not kaffir work; the man must be put in his place.' It was wrong that a Xhosa should be engaged in work of a skilled nature. Why permit this one exception to the rule?

Somewhat against the general tide of opinion, I considered Job Reservation to be the worst of many evils which, combined, made up the total incongruity of apartheid. On this point I was not in agreement with African leaders who saw as Enemy No. 1 the Pass Laws. To my way of thinking, work represents the essence of human existence. The relevance of work remains constant, regardless of the social order, whether primitive or industrialised. Either we hunt or plant, gaining our subsistence from forest or field, or we do our hunting and grubbing in factories, stores and offices. From the African point of view it is easier to campaign against the Pass Laws, which affect everyone, male and female, young and old. This I could understand. But for me as a loner, there was no need to bow to expedience. So I stuck to my guns. My private war was against Job Reservation. It does not depress me to be the odd man out.

To have been proved wrong in the case of the solitary Xhosa employed on the chassis sub-assembly line would have created no offence, but before long my fears were shown to be grounded in fact. One disheartening day, while on my rounds between Body Shop and Trim Final, I noted the absence of my Xhosa friend whose presence had come to be regarded as a ray of hope. Of course he may have been ill, though this was to be doubted. A man of his physique does not crack easily.

Shortly afterwards I came upon him in a different section, remote from the chassis lines. He was not wearing overalls as usual, only an ill fitting apron. Instead of the customary outsize hammer or wrench, he wielded a broom. He used his new tool lethargically. There was no need to question him, but it would have been pointless to engage in small talk. So I asked what had happened, why the demotion?

The burly Xhosa looked down at his feet without answering. I prompted him further.

At length he said; 'The white bosses. They have objected.'

'Job Reservation?'

'Yes.'

The news did not come as a surprise. Even so, the factual revelation shocked me. There is no chance for exaggeration. I felt the blow to the man's pride as surely as if it had hit me.

Upon enquiry his story was substantiated. From a working viewpoint it was no concern of mine, and there were only two approaches open to me. I made them, not halfheartedly, but with despondency. Firstly I spoke to the Production Manager, remarking that there was no staff member more suited to his job than the broad-shouldered Xhosa before his demotion, and what a pity to see a good man slighted, a willing worker wasted. I spoke seriously. This was no occasion for any *Quo Vadis* frivolity.

Later I said my piece to the smug, ineffectual Personnel Manager. I cannot presume that my words had any effect.

A few days later I took the same route, passing Body Shop and Trim Final and arriving at . . . No, it could not be true!

But yes, it was. There, back at his accustomed job, wearing overalls, the makings of a chassis spread out before him, was the Xhosa, smiling broadly. Pride may be a failing, but here was pride at its best.

In a kindlier age it might have been remarked that my heart sang. Something like that did happen. At sight of the beaming black face I went on my way, singing to myself.

This is the beauty and truth of shared experiences. I have felt it in the wilds of primitive Africa, sharing with the creatures of veld and forest their gains and losses. I have realised it where people are involved. Sometimes one is depressed, another time elated. Whichever way it is, one *feels*, one *lives*.

On the other hand, apartheid which means apartness, signifies deprevation, the loss of feeling, of caring for other than oneself.

I wish my story could end here, on a happy note.

But South Africa under apartheid rule is not a fairy-tale land in which all ends happily, with good triumphing over evil. Other forces were at work behind the scenes, vengeful, unrelenting. For the Xhosa it was back to the dull drudgery of the sweeping brush, with an apron to remind him of his proper station in life. For me it was another turn of the screw on the rack of truth, the torture of knowing that good intentions are of no account in a situation fraught with violence.

THE REVOLUTIONARIES

Background:

* 'We live in a country where classic revolutionary conditions are developing.' (Dr Jan Graaff, economist brother of the late Sir De Villiers Graaff, 1965)

* 'Africa is ripe for revolution.' (Premier Chou En-lai, on African visit, June 1965)

* 'Revolution is justified against an oppressive, dictatorial regime which does not allow for change, improvement and development by means of political persuasion.' (Mr John Mendelson, Labour M.P. Plenistowe)

* 'The Afrikaner must beware lest the autocratic power he now wields is wrested from his hands and turned against him.' (Editorial, *Die Beeld*, Afrikaans Press)

* 'The urge to destroy is also a creative urge.' (Mikhail Bakunin)

* 'We think the armed struggle will only end when the causes of the struggle end.' (Samora Machel, 1976)

* 'Blind persistence with separate development will result in full-scale revolution.' (Laurence Gandar, former editor *Rand Daily Mail*, 1976)

* 'Anyone who has doubts as to whether he may demand something he is entitled to has lost the will to struggle for it.' (Naboth Mokgatle)

* 'I would say that the whole life of any thinking African in this country drives him continuously to a conflict between his conscience on the one hand and the law on the other.' (Nelson Mandela)

* 'They have made me what I am and for that I am grateful. This perpetual harassment 24 hours of every day reminds me of my call, of my ideals. Each of these measures of harassment is a test of the strength of my ideals.' (Winnie Mandela)

* 'The twilight of a little freedom is over. We are entering a

period of darkness.' (Dr Nthato Motlana, leader of Soweto's
"Committee of Ten", 1978)

* 'We are working toward full South African citizenship. We
don't want citizenship of a homeland foistered on us. We reject
as well Dr Koornhof's latest idea of dual South African and
homeland citizenship.' (Thozamile Botha, ex-chairman Port
Elizabeth Black Civic Organisation, 1980)

* 'Behind people like myself and Bishop Tutu there is an angry
black youth who says we are delaying change.' (Dr Nthato
Motlana, March 1981)

* 'Can we abandon a country that has stood beside us in every war we've fought, a country that strategically is essential to the free world?' President Reagan said in Washington last night that the U.S. could not abandon South Africa, a wartime ally and producer of essential minerals, and praised the record of many South Africans in trying to erase apartheid. (News report 5th March 1981)

'It seems as if there are changes when in fact the State is merely consolidating its hold over the people. The real change will not come about peacefully because the Nationalists will not change.' (Dr Nthato Motlana, addressing Mowbray Inter-Race Group on 'A New Dispensation for South Africa', Cape, March 1981)

THE REVOLUTIONARIES

We are what we are:

> In our search for truth we sift
>> the sands of time, check the drift
>> of continents, searching
>>>> to what end?

> Life, bounteous though it may be,
>> withholds one sacred mystery,
>> the key to worldly mastery.

> It is life's subtle irony
>> that in our search for truth the key
>> lies in imagery.

We are Revolutionaries:

> We are said to be terrorists
>> and this sounds bad,
>> but we are revolutionaries
>> and this is good.
> We come not to terrorise
>> but to revolutionise.
> Here, where there is apartheid,
>> there is a situation tailor made
>> for revolution. We meet the need.
> And if we die by the sword
>> we rest with honour afterward
>> in non-surrender to a monster greed.

We are Fundamentalists:

> We take the environment
>> to our hearts. Loving the land
>> will it disown us for our stand?

> Be it desert, bush or barren scrub,
>> though exiled and forced to roam,
>> there where our hearts are, is home.

We are essential parts, king-pins
    in a globe that creaks as it spins
    about its axis.

Listen! In deserts you can hear
    our world turn if you keep an ear
    pressed to the ground.

To serried dunes the winds declare
    our intent; not to counter, but dare
    to foster change.

We appear as desperadoes
    gunning to right the wrong,
    siding with the weak against the strong.

We ride roughshod, rude critters,
    hustling, rustling, a hardy breed,
    non-racial, non quitters.

We are mavericks kicking
    against the traces. Too tight a rein
    and we buck the system, to our pain.

We are Radicals:

    Where compromise extends too far
        our aim is not to give and take
        but to make or break.

    When sterile leadership lasts too long,
        frustrating the fruitful offspring of desire
        we abort the wrong.

    Amid corruption that assumes
        a fervour of its own, our fiery
        rage consumes.

    Where government builds a pyre
        of human aspirations
        we snatch the brand and start a fire.

    In lands of shimmering dissent,
        scarred with envy, charred with greed,
        we fan the flames hell-bent.

Dissecting deserts of despair,
   littered with skulls of shrunken hopes,
   we set the torch without a care.

The desert's burning soul reflects
   more than its own seering heat, our dissent
   and soaring discontent.

The mirage dancing in the distance
   mirrors our dejection, refracts, it seems,
   our broken daytime dreams.

The desert waste through which we pass
   portrays a vast desolation,
   prompts our dedication.

It is not easy to turn from plush
   home comforts, lovers, friends,
   and head for bush.

The blazing bowl of fire descends,
   kisses the horizon and departs
   leaving its impress in our hearts.

In wraiths the desert's fiery breath
   mounts with our rage. Your jest in life
   our joust with death.

For we are Revolutionaries:

From earth, from fire,
   from angry gods, from us
   comes the challenge; Change
   or be changed.
To accept or die
   to live or rust?
Change, or as ashes lie
   dust unto dust?

THE SABOTEURS

The two opposing trends of thought:

The ruler and the ruled

the oppressor and the oppressed.

The governing minority

the subdued majority.

Background:

'Saboteurs must be shot out of hand wherever they show themselves.' (Prof. Herman Venter, head of Department of Criminology, University of Pretoria)

'When we wanted to negotiate, they sent everyone who wanted to negotiate into jail. All peaceful means have been exhausted.' (Tsietsi Mashinini, 20, former President, Soweto Students' Representative Council)

'If you want to live by the sword you must perish by the sword.' (Mr Justice Munnick, Supreme Court, Queenstown)

'The war preparations of the South African Government and their constant resort to force has compelled the people to change their tactics.' (Nelson Mandela)

'It is left to the discretion of the courts to impose the death penalty or not.' (Mr B. J. Vorster, Minister of Justice)

'It cannot be expected that people will stop fighting for human rights and dignity, even if death is the penalty.' (Walter Sisulu, former Sec.-General, African National Congress)

'If you wish to protest against the Government it appears to me that this is not the way to do so.' (Mr Justice Bekker, Rand Criminal Sessions, Johannesburg)

'Xintolo urged people to support what he regarded as a freedom struggle in this country. The State might feel that there are existing channels through which he could

'To try to undermine and overthrow the lawfully appointed Government of the country by other than lawful means is a crime of great magnitude.' (Mr Justice A. E. Burger)

'The non-whites will never be allowed the franchise in white South Africa.' (Mr B. J. Vorster, Minister of Justice)

'If South Africa is turned into a hell on earth, then it will be the fault of outside interference.' (Mr J. J. Fouche, Minister of Defence, May 1963)

Four African members of the Pan-Africanist Congress, described as 'hooligans and ruthless murderers who

legally air his grievances. But as far as townsmen like Xintolo are concerned, there is nothing obvious that suggests itself.' (Mr A. L. Sachs, appearing for Xintolo)

'I have believed in passive resistance all my life, but this policy has got us nowhere. I decided to take part in the blowing up of the railway toolshed because it was the only form left to me of retaliating and protesting against the harsh methods of the Government.' (One of three Indians sentenced to ten years imprisonment at Rand Criminal Sessions, Johannesburg, May 1963)

'I have all my life been almost a pacifist. But I think there are occasions when justice and decency can only be upheld by force.' (Mr Patrick Duncan, April 1963)

'We can no longer communicate adequately with the rest of the human race for it does not understand what we are saying and we do not accept what it is saying.' (Mr Laurence Gandar, Editor, *Rand Daily Mail*, July 1965)

Before sentence was passed, Thomas Molathegi (one of the four men) said Pan-Africanism was part of the

would stop at nothing to achieve their aims' were sentenced to death by Mr Justice Ludorf, Rand Criminal Sessions, for the murder of an African special branch detective.

'I sentence you with a prayer in my heart that this period of imprisonment will give you time to contemplate.' (Mr J. L. Cilliers after telling Miss Sylvia Neame that there was a complete absence of repentence and a persistence in her views, and sentencing her to a further two years imprisonment)

'It is a little frustrating only to be able to tackle this very serious moral problem by speech. I'd be more concerned with the action than with the speech.' (Mr Harold Wilson, Labour Party leader, reaffirming his intention to stop shipment of British arms to South Africa)

A 16-year-old African schoolboy stood weeping in the dock of the Pretoria Supreme Court while his father pleaded with Mr Justice P. M. Cillie to show leniency. The Judge, 'After much thought and worry', sentenced the boy to ten years

universal struggle against racial discrimination and he had joined the PAC 'To help water the great tree that would spread its branches all over the world to make men of all races free and equal.' (News report Oct. 2nd 1963)

'Can I doubt my conscience when a civilised world says the same thing?' (Sylvia Brereton Neame, in statement in mitigation)

'Let us then in desperation try sabotage and hope that the world powers in time will realise the seriousness of the situation.' (Mr Walter Sisulu)

'The futile policy of sabotage and violence is a child of despair.' (*Rand Daily Mail*)

imprisonment for conspiring
to commit sabotage. (News
report July 3rd 1963)

'They (non-whites) will not
have political rights in my
fatherland.' (Mr B. J. Vorster
when Deputy Minister of
Education, Arts and Science,
speaking in Port Elizabeth
City Hall, July 28th 1960)

'I myself am an Afrikaner. We
Afrikaners have struggled for a
long time to get economic and
political recognition. You are
also entitled to struggle for
your people, but not to make
use of violence.' (Mr Justice
Snyman, sentencing Mr Joe
Gqabi to ten years imprisonment for a political offence)

'In World War II, certain
South Africans developed the
policy of sabotage against
their fellow countrymen and
women who were serving with
the Allies in defence of their
countries. Bombs were plenti-
ful, particularly in Potchef-
stroom and Johannesburg and
some valuable lives were lost
and much material damage
done. A few saboteurs were
arrested and interned – *not*
executed. (Reader's letter,
Evening Post, Sept. 24th 1965)

'Acts of sabotage are like
writing letters to the
Government.' (John Mosu-
pye, self-confessed cell leader
of *Umkhonto We Sizwe*, giving
evidence at trial of nine Africans charged with sabotage,
Supreme Court, Pretoria,
Aug. 16th 1964)

'The police came and killed
our people. This was done by
the servants of our father (the
Government) our great
mighty father. Tell us where
we can take our complaint to
now.' (Spokesman at Inquiry
into clash at Ngqusa Hill, near
Flagstaff, June 7th 1960,
when police fired and killed
six Pondos and wounded 13
others)

Harris took a long farewell
from his son the day before he
was hanged. (News report
April 3rd 1965)

'I am an African as much as any black man can claim to be.' (Dr De Wet, former South African Ambassador in London, 1965)

'That which belongs to us we did not steal, and for this reason nobody will be allowed to take it out of our hands.' (Mr B. J. Vorster)

'We will have to tell the world that this soil is our own legal right, that God gave it to us, and that no one will snatch it out of our hands.' (Mr B. J. Vorster)

Five months before the vital election of the first Chief Minister of the Transkei in December 1963, the Government concluded a land deal in which a 2,630 morgen farm near Lusikisiki was granted free to Chief Botha Sigcau, Paramount Chief of Eastern Pondoland. (News report Oct. 2nd 1965)

'We settled a country bare.' (Dr H. F. Verwoerd)

'This is our fatherland. We will move for no one.' (Mr B. J. Vorster)

'We are indigenous people of Africa. The land we claim to

'In South Africa we have a handful of wilful men desperately hanging on to power in defiance of the tide of history.' (Emperor Haile Selassie of Ethiopia)

'Mayibuye Africa' – Come back, Africa.

'When the whites came to our country we had the land, they had the bible; now we have the bible and they have the land.' (Origin unknown)

'If the present political lunacy of hard-liners within your regime triumphs, we black and white South Africans may at this very moment be poised for a holocaust of dimensions not witnessed by the world within living memory.' (Chief Gatsha Buthelezi addressing white representatives of South African Government at opening of third sessions of Kwa-Zulu National Assembly)

'We want our land back.' (Poqo oath)

'We want our land back.' (Poqo oath)

'We want our land back.' (Poqo oath)

be ours really belongs to us.'
(Dr Carel de Wet, S.A.
Ambassador, London)

'Who is sabotaging what in this country?'
(Dr A. B. Kazi, executive member, Transvaal Indian Congress)

THE SABOTEURS

Who are the real saboteurs,
whose the crime, where the guilt?

Slowly from his lethargy the slumbrous giant stirs,
    buried in his breast an ember, once a fire.
Reawakened, to what does he aspire
    if not to freedom?

The ashes fanned, he remembers
    odes of old, tales of past glories retold,
    deeds of daring, largely exaggerated,
    feats of war, highly elaborated,
    stories of manhood emerging, where begins
    the chase of maidens, known to be virgins.

O those were the lush days of loose loin cloth
    and supple limbs, of ceremony and rite,
    counsels of war, the scent of victory
    before the closing in of night,
    before the unavoidable fall
    with the assegai subordinate to the gun,
    the tomtom's beat broken by bugle call,
    rivers running red, in torrents sweeping on,
    a body count of ten thousand to one.

No longer the sound of laughter spilling wild
    save from self-indulgent child,
    gone the joy, the thread that ran through everything,
    only the make-believe mouth masking
                    the body's suffering.

106

To what dark truth
                        does an abandoned child awaken?
A world uncaring is readily forsaken.

The child becomes a man, his world of green grasses
    forbidden. Wherever he walks he trespasses;
    he moves among strangers, if move he dares,
    in the land of his forebears.

Where the once proud warriors, bedecked, resplendent?
Gone the pride, gone the splendour, instead the kowtow
                    to masters supposedly benevolent.
Where the medicine men, the rainmakers, the chiefs?
They have made way for new beliefs,
                   and are declared redundant.
Where the tribes trilling, milling,
               meaning to prove their metal?
Vanquished, subdued, they have been herded
             into stockades like cattle.

That which cannot be changed must be endured;
    heavy the heart in captivity.
That which cannot be endured
                must be changed at any cost;
    rare the spirit of bravery.

That which cannot be changed from without
    fashions its own demise from within.
The emperor who declares himself immortal
    acts as his own executioner.

The bare suggestion of permanence
    triggers reaction, invites despair,
    drives some to seek by violence
    what others have sought through prayer.

The mere thought of change forestalls permanence;
    the saboteur starts by breaking down old concepts
    of permanent ways, great walls, pyramids of power;
    the artist in him rebels, depicts

landscapes of desolation,
    the engine throbbing in his heart becomes
    a locomotive running off the rails,
    the kindling of a child deprived
    fires a conflagration in his mind.

We are saboteurs . . .
                    slogan painters,
        writers of open letters
        to crude authority, closed-book government,
        without false preamble – Dear Sirs.
Opportunities have to be made,
        they are not heaven sent.
Militants of a moonless night,
        recruiting words, stepping up the fight,
        we bombard an entrenched State
        with the truth incarnate
        in imagery, allied with brevity.
Writers of peaceful prose,
        preludes to bomb and blast,
        in us resides no facade,
        only the facts relieved of charade.
Letters that should be signed and sent
        under sealed cover we present
        in streaks of orange, yellow, brown,
        on viaducts, on freeways into town,
        on curbstones of a roundabout;
        TO HELL WITH SIGCAU, SELL OUT.

In the midst of purple deeds
        another warning wrung from the heart
        to a world that heeds
        neither the artist nor his art.

For indecent words scribbled on a wall
        there is a token fine or none at all.
For our prim words, one line placed out of bounds,
        it is all or nothing, make or break,
        with life and liberty at stake.

Parapet painters, rebels on the run,
    daub defiant message, day-glo bright,
    daub and dash, duty seen to be done
    before the first streak of morning light.

We are saboteurs . . .
                  train derailers,
    simple strategists who switch
    the points to danger,
    planning to forestall
    tragedy for one and all.

On twin tracks our future is laid out,
    on common sleepers rifts of faith and doubt
    seem to converge, though only distantly;
    broad or narrow the gauge of destiny.

Signals set for strife survey
    diverging points in disarray.
Twisted tortured railroad share
    the iron of our despair.

We see the monster bearing down
    calamity route, the railroad into town.
We see the monster as a train
    and we must slay it or ourselves be slain.

We are saboteurs . . .
                  fire raisers,
    sons of the mighty Shiva,
    traditionalists, hut burners,
    practitioners of an ancient rite,
    a way of setting wrongs to right.

In rare outbursts we aspire
    to divinity. No less do they
    whose faith is in the power of fire
    to cleanse. When all else fails
    fire must have its say.

Into the cauldron of neglect
    we fling our fiery cocktails,
    modernists in this respect.
Whoever despairs of earth and air and water
    still has primeval fire
    for blaze of wrath and righteousness
    and a way to seek redress.

When authority's hands have hardened
    we may join the defeated masses
    and cease from striving, head in sand,
    or we may pluck the burning brand
    and start a conflagration of our own.

Men of little substance, men of water,
    railing, reckless rulers, full of ire,
    greedy, grasping, granting no quarter,
    have made us what we are, men of fire.

Rise, ragged tongues of purifying flame,
    consume the charred and cherished aim;
    hope lies in ashes. Scatter ash and shatter
    all that seemed to matter.

    *   *   *   *

After the lightning flash, the pause
    before the rumbling thunder roll;
    events long past creep up and cause
    hopelessness which then exacts its toll.

Who, then, are the real saboteurs,
    whose the crime, where the guilt?
Did you not extend your sympathy
    to ward off deepening despair,
    you watched the unfolding tragedy
    without a care?

Your hands are clean, you say,
    how clean are they?
You hoped that time might heal
    and so delayed?
You were powerless to act, hamstrung
    or afraid?
Above the voice of protest
    you advocated silence?
You heard a tyrant brag
    and thought it was pretence?
You make pious exhortation
    but admit no moral obligation?
How prudent, how sporting the All Blacks
    playing ball with Springboks, scoring tries
    while Soweto burned, how unwise.
And you the spectator, idling while time flies.

You say, 'We cannot accept the overgrown
    burdens of the world, having enough of our own.'
Yet you receive without demur
    the earth's bounties,
    pelts from animals which occur
    beyond your boundaries,
    rare spices from the East,
    corn from the granaries of the West,
    whale oils and fats from polar regions,
    dates and figs from where they grow best.
In fair balance of trade
    you accept commodities in legions;
    that which cannot be made
    can be bought. Accept then, the boundless
    invigorative sense
    of belonging, of worldliness
    with its duty and recompense.

You should have known, from history's pages,
    how any tyrant, sated with power,
    strides forth and re-engages
    old adversaries. With each revisitation
    we retrogress, lose forward motion,

slip back from advantageous station,
and through recurring chapters make of history
a farce if not a tragedy.

★   ★   ★   ★

Violence proffers no solution,
  offers no reward; this may be true.
But it wipes clean the slate,
  prepares the ground for starting anew.
Hate returned does not cancel hate;
  this also may be true.
But it turns the soiled pages
  of irretrievable past ages,
  makes ready for revision
  sums of unaccountable suffering,
  the ravages of human toil that bring
  depletion born of false division.

The crude canvas of the slogan painter
  is the rough hemp of indifference;
  the train derailer is the child we create
  of poverty, the mail train running late;
  the fire raiser's target, tinder-dry from neglect,
  is the one world from which we cannot defect.

A child grows noticeably in stature
  but how does the secretive mind mature?
How far outgrown is the child who placed
  copper coins of small denomination
  on iron rails, then waited,
  lurking like a grown conspirator,
  sensing his moment of truth with breath abated?
The coins, flattened wafer thin
  were his first sacrificial offering.
Though defaced and not worth much
  they left their mark, the touch
  of suppressed exhultation,
  the stamp of further expectation.

112

To deny all this
   is tantamount to sabotage.

Fate casts its subtle net
   enmeshing all. Then know
   that sins, once deemed scarlet,
   shall be white as driven snow.

The evil projected
   into the Gaderene swine
   is yours and mine.
Let him cast the first stone
   whose aim is true;
   his the power to atone
   for all who follow headlong after
   errant leaders courting disaster.

Personal Reflections

The memory of my headlong flight from Govan Mbeki's office after nearly falling into the arms of two Special Branch members remains vivid and reminds me of a lesser occasion when I endangered myself to no purpose and was saved from the consequences of my folly by an unaccountable change of behaviour. This was at a time when the bombing of selected targets was at its height, though the campaign was amateurish and soon fizzled out. Damage to Government property was the aim, without involving injury or death. The targets were electricity pylons and substations, railway lines, signal boxes. In those early days it was imagined that a few squibs might frighten Government into granting slight concessions that would be better than nothing. It was a forlorn hope to which I could not subscribe. With visions of Verwoerd's Bantustans filling the future, there was no reason for those in power to relinquish their hold, and indeed they were in the process of tightening their grip.

It was a time of deepening despondency for the opponents of apartheid. After the Treason Trial, following Sharpeville and Rivonia, there was need for patience, still more marking of time. Count up to ten, then start again. Into this period of help-lessness there came to my notice a new name, that of a lecturer at Witwatersrand University. His home was situated conveniently in an uncongested part of Port Elizabeth, so I decided to pay him a call, unannounced. It was a case of clutching at straws. I had lost Govan and yearned for someone else politically mature in whom to confide.

There was no parking problem and the number was located readily, on the ground floor of a block of flats, quite modern. So far, so good. The sound of typing was clearly audible. Luckily, someone was at home. Presumably the lecturer I had come to see was hard at work trying to unravel the tangled skein of apartheid. Through the glass panelled front door a man could be seen in shadowy form seated before a typewriter. The sound of voices mingled with the staccato clack-clack-clack of the typewriter, pounded at speed.

There was no answer to my first knock. The typing continued without interruption. Hesitating for a few moments, I knocked a second time. Again there was no response. Pausing, I raised my hand to knock a third time.

With hand held aloft there came a change of mind. Instead of knocking, I turned and walked away. What prompted me is difficult to say. Usually I am dogged, tenacious as a terrier. It would have been more in keeping with my nature to have gone on knocking until the door was opened.

What swayed me on this occasion? What made me go against my normal inclination, my mission unfulfilled? Most people would have knocked just once more, if only to play up to the superstition of third time lucky.

Why were my knocks not answered? Why did I not knock again? We speak of free will. To what extent do we possess it? Half flippantly, we speak of guardian angels. Was mine watching over me at this time?

I ask, because a week later there came the news of a police raid on this man's home. An arrest was made following the discovery of materials for the manufacture of time delay bombs. Shortly afterwards, with a haste calculated to serve as a deterrent to others, the ex-University lecturer was brought to trial and sentenced to a lengthy term of imprisonment, twelve years if I remember rightly. Innocents suffered too. Behind the scene was a young wife with a baby only a few weeks old. The child would not know its father as a free man until so late in life that the two must remain comparative strangers to one another. For there would be no remission of sentence. Never is there any reduced term when the name of the culprit denotes a non-Afrikaner or the skin colour happens to be wrong, or when the deed is politically motivated against the perpetuation of white privilege.

What had compelled this man of learning to commit an act of folly so doomed to failure? There can be no accounting for the deeds of others. If we cannot live with them through all the vicissitudes, the ups and downs of life, then we cannot expect to piece together the successes and failures which are their lot and not ours. The closest we can come to understanding their motives is to question the course of fate. If only this man had taken time off from teaching . . . if only he had sought a clearer concept, preferably alone . . . if only he had heeded the still, calm voice within . . .

I sought to analyse my own actions similarly. If only I had knocked a third time . . . If I had been my ordinary self, persistent to a degree . . . if I had met and talked with this man, to share with him his knowledge of explosive devices . . .

How thankful I am not to have become an accomplice, a partner in an act of sheer stupidity ending in jail. On such slender threads of chance does one's future depend. In my better moments I have felt a deep humility. It stems from the knowledge that I represent a part and not the whole. My role cannot be that of a Govan Mbeki and should not be that of a man seeking to hasten history, which is long in unfolding. To usurp too wide a responsibility is to stand the chance of wrecking what little good might be accomplished. The time is not yet ripe for drastic change. Continuing patience is the order of the day. Naught, as yet, for comfort.

Looking back, as now, I am grateful for this experience and to have it remain so small. Perhaps, as poet and historian, more can be achieved . . .

THE INFORMERS

Background:

* Bigger rewards, more police and the public's co-operation are features of a new police plan against sabotage. Lt-Gen. J. M. Keevy said that the R1,000 reward for information of saboteurs announced last week would conceivably be increased even by several thousand rand where the circumstances warranted it. Lt-Gen. Keevy appealed to members of the public to watch out for suspicious-looking persons and to report the first sign of sabotage to the nearest police station immediately. (News report 3rd Dec. 1962)

* 'In the case of sabotage we are prepared to increase the reward. Any information that is good will be rewarded.' (Commissioner of Police, 3rd Dec. 1962)

* The Head of the C.I.D., Major-General R. J. van den Bergh, confirmed that the police are offering a reward of R50 for information which led to the arrest of a leader of a Poqo cell anywhere in South Africa. He said that to date the offer of a reward had had a 'favourable reaction.' (News report 22nd March 1963)

* Col. J. Rossouw, Divisional Commissioner of Police for the Transkei, warned Africans against the Poqo movement and advised them to get in touch with the police or a Bantu Commissioner secretly if they had information on Poqo. He said that the identity of Africans who did this would be kept secret and that they would enjoy police protection. (News report 22nd May 1963)

* An African who accused another of Poqo activities to get the R50 reward offered by the State was sentenced to six months imprisonment, without the option of a fine. It was a very low type of crime and the other African could have received the death penalty for the R50 that Madumelwana Tsoni of Bochabella Village, Bloemfontein, wanted to get fraudulently, said the magistrate. (News report 14th May 1963)

* A spirit of fear and restlessness has gripped African townships in the Eastern Cape. Fear of unidentified African

police informers is widespread. Political meetings have suddenly stopped. Many people first look round before talking about politics. They say the telephones are tapped. (Comment in Cape newspaper, June 1963)

* A headless body believed to be that of a former member of the banned African National Congress was found in Kabah location recently. Mr Moses Botomani disappeared from his home about two weeks ago. 'It was usual for him at times to stay away from home for long periods,' said his wife. 'He never explained his absences.' (News report 29th June 1963)

* A police informer was murdered in Kanye location in Engcobo district on Saturday night, a senior police officer said. (News report 20th Aug. 1963)

* Police hopes are high that the record reward of R4,000 offered for information will lead to the arrest of the four escaped 90-day detainees (Arthur Goldreich, Harold Wolpe, Mosie Moola and Abdulhai Jassat). It is hoped it will tempt informers. (News report 21st Aug. 1963)

* The witness, known as Witness F to protect him from retaliation, said he belonged to the African National Congress. An earlier witness – known as Witness E – said that he, too, belonged to the A.N.C. (News report 15th Jan. 1964)

* The Rev. Dr Henri Junod, a prison chaplain in this country for nearly thirty years, was banned from visiting prisons after being accused of 'fostering African nationalism' among prisoners. He denied the allegations, yet the prisons remained closed to him and he left South Africa without knowing who his accusers were. (News report April 1964)

* A reward of several thousand rand is reported to have been offered for information leading to the capture of Wilton Makwayi, 'the last known African leader' who had not been detained, banned, arrested, or who had not left the country, until his arrest in October 1964. The main State witness at the Rivonia Trial, Mr X, said during the trial that Makwayi was living in Rivonia for several months before the raid. (News report 22nd Oct. 1964)

* Mr Berrange put it to Beyleveld that he was either a perjurer or a traitor. 'Did you read what the Judge-President called Adrian Leftwich? (Mr Justice A. B. Beyers, in a Cape Town trial which ended yesterday, said Leftwich was an insult to the genus *rattus* – to the rat species). Do you fall into that category?' (Trial of Abram Fischer and 13 others on charges under the Suppression of Communism Act, Nov. 1964)

* 'A seed of great bitterness has been sown inside me. I certainly hope there will be a time when these people against whom I am giving evidence can forgive me.' (Adrian Leftwich, after long cross-examination at trial of his former colleagues, Cape Town, Nov. 1964)

* Ramsingh Behari, 21, placed four sticks of dynamite, a length of safety fuse and two detonators in the offices of the Natal Indian Congress in Lakhani Chambers and then reported the matter to the Security Police. He hoped to be paid a reward for the information. But yesterday he was found guilty of fraud by Mr M. E. Goodhead in the Durban Regional Court. (News report 4th Dec. 1964)

* Mr Isaacson (defence counsel at trial of Dr Masilomoney Pather in Port Elizabeth Regional Court) said the State witnesses who described a meeting in Pather's home had given evidence in a 'parrot-like fashion.' The gravest doubt should be cast on evidence of this nature. Some of the evidence was 'absurd' he said. (News report 28th July 1965)

* The advocate, Mr D. Soggot, questioned an African witness about the new clothes he was wearing. The witness, identified only as 'D', was brought back and Mr Soggot asked him where he had got the clothes. The witness pointed out Sgt. J. du Preez, of the Port Elizabeth Security Branch as the man who had given him the clothes. (Trial of Miss Sylvia Neame, Humansdorp, May 1965)

* A State witness testified that the three accused had attended a Poqo meeting in Molteno at which he had been present. When questioned by the accused (who conducted their own defence) the witness denied that he had been beaten by the police or that he had been given a pair of trousers by a policeman. (Trial of

two African brothers, one aged 17, Port Elizabeth Regional
Court, 27th Aug. 1965)

* 'The Rivonia Raid in the Transvaal came as a direct result of
information received from people held under the so-called No
Trial Act.' (Mr B. J. Vorster)

* 'Throughout history you always find collaborators, the weak
oppressed joining with their oppressors.' (Peter Hain)

THE INFORMERS

Why, why, why . . .
          for pieces of silver, thirty,
          for rand fifty only . . .

          Why so great a perfidy?
          Why, for so little reward?
          Why the loss of peace within,
             sacrificed of your own accord?
          Why the resultant insecurity,
             why the incessant prick
             of conscience for a mite,
             barely enough to buy a toothpick,
             revenue for a song of hate?
          Is life that cheap,
             are we but ants,
             trampling one another, so degraded
             that information can be traded
             for a pair or worn, soiled pants?

          Life may let us down, we may reap
             the whirlwind, but Brother,
             why this from one to another?
          Disloyalty, treachery,
             these will ever be,
             but why, why at so low a price,
             basement bargain for so much malice?

Why, why, why . . .
    may as well ask a spy
      to account for treason.
    Product of the soil, rich or poor,
      labour of love or wearisome toil,
      so the crop in due season.

    Informers are seldom seen
      except in court; seldom seen
      even in court, their anonymity shrouded
      by hood of shoulder length,
      black as their misdeeds are clouded.
    Hirelings, returning home they are
      the richer by how much?
    Mercenaries, going home
      the poorer by far.
    Collaborators, sometimes in the night
      dealt with summarily
      out of court
      and serves them right.
    Headfirst they emerged from the womb,
      let them go headlong to their doom,
      appropriate end for modern Judas,
      eternal knave who flits across the stage
      in this and every toilworn age.
    Judas, Judas, what a lowly part to play
      in the tragi-comedy
      of this our day.

    Ssh! Do not raise your voice.
    Ssh! Do not talk so loud.
    Speak in whispers or not at all –
      this the better choice.
    The courtroom makes a banquet of the proud;
      our only safety is a shroud
      of silence from cockcrow to nightfall.
    Be careful when you use the telephone,
      I'm sure the line is tapped.
    Don't wait for allegations
      of Witness 'A'

or the sworn revelations
of Agent 'Q',
the next to be trapped
may be YOU.
Beware the chance acquaintance
and in his presence
the gesture of perchance.
Beware the casual stranger
and the incautious, casual word,
likewise the w-h-i-s-p-e-r
waiting to be overheard.
Beware the surly, silent stalker
ex-scrum half, now Special Branch,
who awaits but half a chance.
Better beware of all, of him, of her.

Ssh! It does not pay to think aloud.
Ssh! It does not pay to think at all.
    Then go your way
        silent as a passing cloud.

Judas, Judas returned, what brings you here,
    Judas, Judas, whom to betray
    for so little? What lurking fear
    compels, how tortuous the dismay?

Covert, cunning, clinging to the shadows,
    shifty, sidling, slinking up to corners,
    keeping step with cortège mourners,
    mingling with the waiting workers,
    nudging, edging into conversation,
    devouring scraps of information,
    furtive on the fringe of congregation,
    peering, prying on lover's trysts,
    courting the next betrayal.

Covert killers, coming from behind,
    vultures of the human race,
    guileless, artless, showing no trace
    of pity, preying on their own kind

not for food or raiment
    but for thirty pieces
    in payment.
Two arms, two legs, two eyes
    but inhuman otherwise.
Pit and trap and snare,
    thirsting for the kill,
    hunting without skill,
    killing without a care.

Shame not the beasts to call them brute,
    and when they die inter with them
                    their worldly loot.

       *   *   *   *

You wonder Why . . .
        and now call me Brother,
        who barely recognised The Other.

The mansion on the hilltop,
    the hovel out of sight below
    and in between a no-man's land.

Multi-storied block of flats
    rising from the inner city,
    landlords settled in a scenic suburb
    within striking distance, sitting pretty.

And somewhere, filed away about tenth storey,
    a captive cipher, coded, computerised,
    regularised and trivialised,
    in milling motion, ant-like,
    wanting to survive, waiting to be trampled.

You who make of money a god,
    within your hearts of stone
    lies the kernal of unbelief.

To whom do we atone,
    for whom your miserly grief;
    closed the bible closed the book,
    locked the heart and kept locked.
The cold drip of dispensed charity
    comes as poor recompense
    for aeons of neglect.
The pious seek salvation from above:
    so do we;
    losers, ar'n't we all?
While you sing its praise the dove
    of peace, goodwill and love
    wings its way and is gone.
Buzzard, falcon, eagle, owl,
    monkish beneath a sort of cowl,
    have talons for supportive need,
    not for supplementary greed.

Yours the substance, yours the show,
    ours but the fallen shadow.
In essence, who the master, who the slave,
    in truth, who the Judas, who the knave?

Background Comment

The Fiercest Fight and the bitterest. A deeply disturbing factor
in the South African liberation struggle against minority rule,
against racist dictatorship, has been the high incidence of
informers and State witnesses. In any struggle there must be
opposition – the struggle presupposes this. But why the
struggle within? Why a treacherous, traitorous element? To say
that poverty plays its part, and in this instance plays a higher
role than usual because of the extremes of wealth and poverty
involved, only serves to cloud the issue. For there is something
more, reaching beyond poverty, beyond racism, beyond
nationalism.

Even Nelson Mandela was betrayed by an informer. Also the
Rivonia Trial accused were informed against, and they represented the big names of African nationalism. Why?

An organising secretary of the African National Congress, Port Elizabeth area, was found to be an informer. A stage was reached when personal vendettas were in vogue. As a consequence, fear was everywhere. I felt it for myself. A ludicrous situation arose of talking in whispers, of making sidelong glances habitually. There had to be a careful sounding out of the company one kept. Not only strangers were suspect, but friends. It became too dangerous to hold political meetings in private homes. Among blacks, funerals made a cover for political gatherings until this ruse also was defeated by infiltration of informers.

Then came the State witnesses, some of them professionals to the extent that they went from court to court, earning for themselves the sobriquet of "travelling witnesses". Some became so used to their roles that they lapsed into lackadaisical, parrot-like performances.

Increasingly large rewards were offered as bait. Even so, the amounts remained comparatively small. The depth of depravity was reached when life with freedom was traded for pairs of second-hand trousers. Throughout the dark and dreadful 1960s something was radically wrong. But what?

Defeatism permeated the atmosphere. Defeatism deep and lasting. Perhaps this provides the answer. From the time of Blood River there had been nothing but defeat. Following the most devastating of military defeats came a modern form of slavery endorsed by racist legislation culminating in apartheid. Loss of land, liberty, dignity. Loss upon loss, and not a glimmer of hope. Defeat, persecution, abandonment.

Most devastating of all was the latter, the knowledge that no help could be expected from outside. The wealthy western democracies found the existing state of affairs profitable, desirable. The Soviet Union, lacking a base in Africa, was in no position to help. Cuba had yet to show its hand, briefly. Colonialism remained strongly entrenched. Angola and Mozambique continued as Portuguese provinces and there seemed no likelihood of change within twenty, thirty years or more. UDI, Unilateral Declaration of Independence, curtained the scene in Rhodesia. South-West Africa became recognised as Namibia, begrudgingly and on paper only.

Chaotic conditions in parts of Africa where independence

had been gained, particularly Ghana, the Congo and Nigeria, played into the hands of those who sought to oppose change. Farther afield, in war-torn Viet Nam, flame throwers, napalm bombs and defoliants gave clear warning to others – and a body count of at least ten to one in favour of those vested with technological superiority.

In South Africa itself, the tight, unrelenting grip of the militarised police made it fairly easy for informers to operate without fear of reprisal. Verwoerd's mesmeric power was at its peak. The Bantustans were taking shape, and come what may, the scrambled egg could not be unscrambled.

Defeatism stretched into the far distant future. Not a single black leader retained his liberty. All had been dealt with effectively. Prison torture was known to be commonplace. Suicides while under interrogation were on the increase, making them suspect – suicide or murder? As though to increase the agony, economic boom conditions prevailed in South Africa – *Alles vir Blankes*.

As yet there were no modern martyrs, non-white. No martyrs and thus no one in whom to place implicit trust. Altogether it was a situation of no hope, a breeding ground for informers, those pitiable wretches, driven by envy, who grow impatient of the winter cold and cannot last out the hour till midnight.

Forgive them, for they know not what they do. Father forgive them.

THE INTIMIDATORS

Background:

* One of the few remaining English-speaking lecturers at the University College of Fort Hare resigned this week as a result of interference of an intimidatory nature by Special Branch detectives in his private and professional life. An incident last week-end when police searched his car, his purse and his pockets on the open road near Breakfastvlei was the final cause of his decision. (News report 21st Oct. 1960)

* 'It must be assumed that the object of the arrests was purely intimidatory, aimed at frightening those who were arrested into accepting Government policies or frightening into inactivity members of the party who were not arrested.' (Mr Peter Brown, Liberal Party national chairman, in statement to effect that during the 1960 State of Emergency a number of Liberal Party members were imprisoned)

* 'We have been imprisoned now for periods of up to a month and more. Yet no person has to date told us the reason for our arrest or confronted us with any charge or allegation or informed us of the period of our confinement.' (Excerpt from petition signed by twelve men detained under emergency regulations, 1960)

* Hundreds of non-whites were rounded up today in the start of a Union-wide mass police drive. (News report May 1961)

* The Secretary of the Congress of Democrats said that the ban on Miss Gillian Jewell, a lecturer in French at the University of Cape Town, was the 64th such ban imposed on members of the Congress. 'The aim is quite clearly to hinder us from advocating our policy of full and equal rights for all South Africans.' (News report 8th Dec. 1961)

* 'I hope the Government will not succeed in so intimidating the different groups that they will not fight for the rights that are theirs. There is a subtle form of intimidation going on and the whites are more intimidated than the Africans – they have so much more to lose.' (Prof. Z. K. Matthews, in farewell message before his departure in April 1962)

* Today's issue of the weekly newspaper *Spark*, successor to the banned *New Age*, will be the last. Earlier this month, the Minister of Justice served banning orders on key members of the staff, banning them from premises at which a publication is compiled, printed or published. A spokesman said, 'The entire editorial staff has been squeezed out by bannings.' (News report 28th March 1963)

* Five banning orders were served last night on a Durban African, Amos Mngome, by Security Branch police. The bannings take effect from today and are for the next five years. (News report 12th April 1963)

* 'The impression seems to be getting around that there is a purge on against Africans.' (Brig. G. J. Joubert, Acting Chief of C.I.D., 26th July 1963)

* Canon James Calata, 68, priest-in-charge of St James' Mission, Cradock, has been prohibited from attending meetings and social gatherings for five years. Canon Calata was installed as the first African canon in the Diocese of Grahamstown in November 1959. (News report 27th July 1963)

* Mrs Girlie Loza said in an affidavit before the Judge-President, Mr A. B. Beyers, in the Supreme Court, Cape Town, that it was obvious that prison and police officials were playing some kind of "cat-and-mouse" game with her husband, Mr Elijah Loza, a 90-day detainee, who was released and then re-arrested. (News report 13th Aug. 1963)

* Looking haggard and drawn, Mrs Wolpe said she had been interrogated 'non-stop' for 17 hours. She was arrested at her Fairwood, Johannesburg, home a few hours after her husband, attorney Mr Harold Wolpe, was discovered missing. Mrs Wolpe said she was often threatened with violence and 'was terrified' of what would happen. 'Once a man came into the room and began to draw the curtains. Another man came in and shouted, "I want to deal with her myself!" This sort of intimidation kept on happening. The two men pulled up chairs close to where I was sitting. They began shouting at me and one held up his hands which were trembling and screamed, "I will throttle you!"' (News report 15th Aug. 1963)

* 'Just as I screamed, the Lieutenant came into the room and laughed at me. "How do you like the treatment?" I was asked. The Lieutenant told the policeman that when they had finished with me they would take a statement from me.' (Complaint by African student, 18, said by the police to be a Pan-Africanist Lieutenant)

* 'If these comparatively light sentences do not have the desired effect, future courts might well decide that the death sentence is necessary.' (Mr Justice Claassen, passing sentence of a total of 79 years imprisonment for sabotage on eight Africans, Supreme Court, Pretoria, 19th Sept. 1964)

* Prof. Edward Roux, one of South Africa's leading scientists and head of the Department of Botany at the University of the Witwatersrand, has been silenced by ministerial order. A series of banning orders which took effect yesterday prohibit him from entering any educational institution, or teaching anyone, or publishing any writings – whether scientific or political. For the next five years, Prof. Roux is also prohibited from entering any location or township reserved for Africans, Coloureds or Asians, or any factory, attending a gathering – even a purely social one – attending any court of law unless he is required as a witness and talking or writing to any other banned person. Prof. Roux has also been confined to the Johannesburg Magisterial Area. He will, therefore, be unable to visit his farm at Muldersdrift, near the City. (News report 17th Dec. 1964)

* A banning order has been served on Dr H. J. Simons, Associate Professor of Comparative African Government at the University of Cape Town, at his holiday home at Onrusrivier, near Hermanus. The order served on him is almost identical with that served on Prof. Edward Roux. (News report 23rd Dec. 1964)

* Mr Tommy Ntoyakhe Charlieman, of Uitenhage, was arrested on May 14, 1963, and was not released till December 9, 1964. He was held at various times in Port Elizabeth, Walmer, Uitenhage and Somerset East jails. His attorney said today as far as he knew no formal charge against the man was ever put to him. Now Mr Charlieman has written to the Minister of Justice, Mr B. J. Vorster, claiming damages for loss of health

and wages. During his absence his wife and younger children were supported by his older children and friends. (News report 30th Jan. 1965)

* Three representatives of the Special Branch with a search warrant visited the office of the *Evening Post* on Friday afternoon. For an hour and 15 minutes they inspected the reference bookshelves, filing cabinet, desk papers, clippings, letters and various journals in the office of the Editor, Mr J. G. Sutherland. After that they made a 15-minute search in the office of the Editor's Secretary. (News report 30th Jan. 1965)

* Politically experienced people who follow trends in South African politics have predicted that 1965 will see the launching of a determined intimidation campaign. This belief is based partly on hints that have been dropped by Mr B. J. Vorster, Sen. De Klerk and others. (Editor, *Saturday Evening Post*, 30th Jan. 1965)

* The *Daily Despatch* yesterday commented on the political police search of the offices of the Editor of the *Evening Post* at the end of last week. The newspaper said; 'If the searching of the offices of the *Evening Post* by the Special Branch was intended to intimidate that newspaper, it was doomed to failure from the start. There is no more courageous editor in the country than Mr John Sutherland.' (2nd Feb. 1965)

* Nearly thirty members of the Liberal Party of South Africa have been banned during the past few months. Among the persons banned – and prohibited from taking any further part in Liberal Party affairs – are; Mr Peter Brown, National Chairman; Mr Randolph Vigne, National Deputy Chairman; Mr Peter Hjul, Chairman of the Cape Division; Mr Barney Zackon who succeeded Mr Hjul as Cape Chairman, and three Cape Deputy Chairmen, Mr Joseph Nkatlo, Mr Terence Beard and Miss Ann Tobias. (News report 20th March 1965)

* Security police raided the offices of the South African Congress of Trade Unions in Johannesburg. They took away about 200 documents. Eleven detectives spent nearly five hours searching the offices. Among the papers they confiscated were cash books, ledgers, bank statements, cheque books and

pamphlets. Sactu is a co-ordinating body of African trade unions which the Government does not recognise. (News report 29th April 1965)

* Canon James Arthur Calata, 70, was sentenced to a years imprisonment for failing to report to the police in terms of a banning order under the Suppression of Communism Act. Apart from four days, the whole sentence was suspended on condition that he is not convicted of any further offence under the Act. (News report 15th May 1965)

* At least ten Port Elizabeth non-white men and women charged with contravening the Suppression of Communism Act have been held in jail for periods ranging from nine to thirteen months without trial. This was revealed by a spokesman for an association which is caring for the detained non-whites families, many of whom, according to the spokesman, are suffering because their breadwinners are in jail. The spokesman said there were probably other non-whites who had been in jail on charges under the Suppression of Communism Act for equally long periods without trial. The association had just 'not been told' about them. (News report 17th June 1965)

* Miss Gillian Jewell, who is banned under the Suppression of Communism Act, had an air-gun pellet fired through her second storey flat window in Sea Point yesterday. On October 18 last year, Mr Peter Hjul, banned Chairman of the Western Cape branch of the Liberal Party, and Mr Fred Carneson, had .22 bullets fired through windows in their homes in Sea Point and Oranjezicht respectively. (News report 18th Jan. 1965)

* Security police conducted a two-hour raid on the Athlone advice office which is run jointly by the Black Sash and the S. A. Institute of Race Relations. They took the names of Africans who had come for advice and went away with files and documents. Staffed by voluntary Black Sash workers, it was established some years ago to help Africans bewildered by the maze of laws surrounding their lives. Dr Oscar Wolheim, M.P.C., Chairman of the Institute in Cape Town, called the raid 'intimidation'. He thought the raid was quite unnecessary as the police had all the information. 'It may be that they are trying to put off

the Africans who seek advice and the women who give it.' (News report 8th July 1965)

* 'It is time that members of the Anglican Church deal with their political bishops.' (Mr B. Schoeman, Minister of Transport)

* 'Our problem is that there are so many people who stick their noses into our affairs. And people do this only where their own affairs don't smell too good.' (Mr B. J. Vorster)

* 'In conclusion I should like to inform you that we do not recognise the right of any foreign organisation or government to interfere in the domestic policies of our country.' (South African Ambassador in London, in reply to Amnesty International's report on prison conditions in South Africa)

THE INTIMIDATORS

Many are the inducements
      to inactivity
  from the Buddha
  to the Bible:

'All action leads to suffering' –
  and the wheel of life spins
  restlessly about a tired world.

'Vanity of vanities, all is vanity' –
  meanwhile the power to corrupt
  mounts up.

   *   *   *   *

Beware the provocations
        of false prophets:

'This means peace in our time' –
    but what if it should bring
    a rude awakening?

'You've never had it so good' –
    and the gullible, believing,
    become the mourners, grieving.

   ★   ★   ★   ★

Insidious are the instigations
            to dalliance:

'South Africa needs time' –
    with the audience held captive
    the show goes on.

'What the Republic needs is time' –
    the privileged exhibit this pretence,
    the possession of patience.

'Give me six months' –
    always more time
    for the perfect crime.

   ★   ★   ★   ★

Subtle are the blandishments
        of the self-righteous:

'Let's give it a try' –
    yes, experiment
    with Bantustans as pie in the sky
    and people as nuclear effluent.

      ★   ★   ★   ★

Soporific are the allurements
            of the *status quo*:

'I'm all right, Jack' –
    the wealthy, the elderly, the young conservative
    prefer things the way they are,
    no change, all take, no give.

'*Alles sal reg kom*' –
    all will come right, apart
    from the inside of jails, with interrogation,
    plus torturers perfecting their art.

      ★   ★   ★   ★

Unyielding the proponents
            of the hard line:

'We must be like granite, not to yield' –
    the heart when steeled
    gives nothing of itself.

'We will move for no one' –
    no less relentless is the tide
    sweeping in, pitiless as human pride.

      ★   ★   ★   ★

Nothing is vain
                    except inaction,
        nothing vain
                    except submission.
All, all is suffering,
    to live is to suffer.
So greet the pain,
    go out and meet it.

Nothing is quite so vain
    as bland indifference,
    nothing quite so vain
    as tame surrender.

Unless we make our presence known
    our absence will be presumed;
Unless we proclaim our strength
    our weaknesses will be apparent;
Unless we protect our rights
    our privileges too, will vanish.

Sources of Quotations

All action leads to suffering. (The Buddha)
Vanity of vanities, all is vanity. (The Bible)
This means peace in our time. (Mr Neville Chamberlain)
You've never had it so good. (Mr Harold Macmillan)
South Africa needs time. (Mr Clarence Randall, US economic adviser)
What the Republic needs is time. (Dr H. F. Verwoerd)
Give me six months . . . (Mr B. J. Vorster)
Let's give it a try. (Field Marshall Lord Mongomery)
I'm all right, Jack. (Common English saying)
Alles sal reg kom. (All will come right, common Afrikaans saying)
We must be like granite, not to yield. (Dr H. F. Verwoerd)
We will move for no one. (Mr B. J. Vorster)

134

One Saturday morning while typing in my study, my wife opened the front door to a man whose authoritative knock brooked no delay. I had heard his footsteps crunching on the loose gravel as he made the long approach to our house, set far back from the road. The unfamiliar strident steps, the tone of voice, alerted me to danger. An animal instinct was at work. I could not hear what was being said, but guessed from the brevity of conversation punctuated by awkward silences that all was not well.

My wife, not easily upset, was agitated when she appeared. A few words were all she could whisper. The man was a member of the Special Branch and I was to go with him to Swartkops police station, there to be fingerprinted.

A minute or so later I stood face to face with a man who exuded "Special Branch" without needing to reveal his identity. In fact he did not declare himself and I did not think to query his authority. He asked me to follow him and there seemed no sense in disobeying, so obvious was his calling. Careful not to offend, he was almost frighteningly polite. While there was nothing in my shady past to warrant criminal record to the extent of fingerprinting, I was so taken off guard as to follow like a dog at heel.

The man had parked his car outside the rear gateway. He wore plain clothes and the car, a Volkswagen, bore no markings to denote that it was a Government vehicle. As we set off, I was assured that the process of fingerprinting would not take long. It was a formality, that was all.

A formality? Fingerprinting? In what age were we living, that it could be declared a formality? With computers just coming into fashion, was this already the age of Big Brother?

There was little conversation as we left Redhouse and motored alongside the Swartkops Salt Company workings, then crossed the bridge leading to the main road bisecting the village of Swartkops. No doubt the Special Branch man felt embarrassed, while I, no glib talker at the best of times, could think of nothing to say. My brain was clouded and would not work. Consequently it took a seeming eternity to cover the short distance. Then, turning left, we arrived at the centrally situated, unimposing police station, so new as to be barely furnished. I must have been one of its first delinquent customers.

Passing through the charge room, where there were two uniformed policemen, I was led into a small room at the rear, which we had to ourselves without interruption. A buff form was produced, printed on both sides; onto this went names, date and place of birth, a lot of rigmarole. Then I was escorted into an anti-room where the serious business of fingerprinting got under way. Not long? A mere formality? Instead, a job that could have been completed within minutes was stretched to one hour, two hours, and still we were hard at it. I had given little thought to fingerprinting hitherto, firm in my opinion that it was no concern of mine. If anything, I imagined it to be a rubber stamp process, a dab or two, and finish. It involved impressions of the index fingers, that was all.

Certainly I had not expected thumb prints to be required as well. But so they were. Instead of a few quick dabs of marking ink and a couple of impressions on a piece of plain paper, I was given the fullest possible treatment. No bank robber, no smash-and-grab thief, no rapist could have been subjected to a more thorough procedure. Apart from this, the messiness was beyond all reckoning. Soon my fingers were in a worse state than those of a four-year-old dabbling with black poster paint for the first time. Every finger, of both hands in turn, were subjected to the same gooey treatment. Both thumbs also. The Special Branch man was painstaking in his search for perfection. Taking into account his limited field of expressionism, he was an artist of no mean calibre. He worked slowly, laboriously. He became so engrossed in his task that he spoke rarely or not at all. Shocked and bewildered, I said nothing. Otherwise I may have protested as he grasped each finger and pressed it firmly onto the buff form. Given time in which to gather my scattered wits, anger would have surfaced.

The first impressions were too blotchy, or in some other way failed to meet the high standard of perfection that was the minimum requirement. If this assumption is correct, the fault was that of the Special Branch man for using too much of the filthy goo. It spread like the plague, proliferated like a weed. Even so, it seemed incredible when the first buff form, complete in every detail, was screwed into a tight ball and tossed into a waste paper basket. But so it was. The whole sorry business was an act, of course.

A second start was made. This time, greater pressure was applied as each finger and thumb was pressed down, but slightly less of the indelible ink was used. Again the long, purposely protracted process. Once more the heavy silence broken only by the man's deep breathing, an essential part of the overall act. By this time I had tumbled to the truth that something more than fingerprinting was involved. I was being subjected to a special kind of intimidation. Well into the second hour, and I was convinced of this. The intention was to frighten me into submission. It was not enough that my fingerprints should be taken within ten or fifteen minutes. My criminality must be stressed, my freedom of movement and expression must be limited by the knowledge that, at police headquarters, officialdom would be able to keep tabs on me. For any political crime in the future, I would be suspect. I had been branded.

To have protested would have been vain and useless. Worse, it would have played into the man's hand. It would have presented him with a chance to gloat. Through my silence, he could hurt me no more than he had done already.

At long last the dirty deed was done. Our relationship having deteriorated, I was told curtly to wash my hands at a tiny washbasin quite inadequate for the purpose. There was no hot water and the soap would not lather. The tarry mess remained indelible. Nevertheless I lodged no complaint, made no request. The glum Special Branch man did nothing to help, having lost interest.

No wonder he did not offer to shake hands when he dropped me outside the front garden gate at home. It is a South African custom to do so; it is almost a fetish. Rivals will shake hands, bitter enemies too. In happier walks of life I have received handshakes from men setting off on week-end trips and handshakes upon their return. At the least provocation Afrikaners will shake hands with non-Afrikaners, providing they are not black. Apartheidists will shake hands with anti-apartheidists. Yet the Special Branch man, though remaining courteous, made no attempt to bid farewell in the traditional manner. I glanced at my hands and knew why.

In the safety of home the truth dawned slowly. It is a kindly provision of nature that time should be required for realisation of deep hurt, whether physical or mental. There was an occasion when I was struck by a passing motor cycle and felt no immediate effect except for a slight numbness in one hand, thrown up in a forlorn gesture of defence. I carried on my way, reached home and went to bed. Nothing appeared to be wrong apart from an aching hand and bruised knee. Upon rising the following morning my legs gave way and I crumpled to the floor. The sense of shock had overtaken me that long afterwards. On the occasion of the fingerprinting it was the same. The sense of shock grew with time.

Eventually the inkstains wore off. The embarrassment and indignation faded gradually. Remaining are two buff forms filed away at police headquarters. They bear an untidy collection of squiggly lines. To what purpose? To whose lasting benefit? Clearly, the object of the exercise was to intimidate, to frighten, to make of me a political nonentity. In this it failed. I am not that type of man. All it did was harden my resolve.

More than ever I saw that apartheid must be rooted out, destroyed. In the nature of things this may involve violence. Nothing of such magnitude is accomplished without intense struggle. Sacrifice is invoked. So be it.

Then whose the guilt? Whose the fingerprints on the pages of history?

Personal Reflections
(2)

It was essential to the purpose of fingerprinting that I should be at home when the Special Branch man called. Otherwise no fingerprints, no intimidation. Therefore he made his call on a Saturday morning. On a later occasion it was preferable that I should not be available to disrupt proceedings. So the call was made on a working day, when my wife was at home but I was not. There were two men on this occasion; it must have been anticipated that there would be a lone woman about the house, so for the sake of propriety there must be two men. They were both broad shouldered, burly, unsmiling fellows, I was told,

138

dressed inconspicuously in plain clothes. This tallied with my assessment of Special Branch men as conforming to a pattern, like peas in a pod. Whatever the total strength of the squad assigned to Port Elizabeth, it could be accepted that all were identical in figure and face, erect, stern, without a trace of good humour. I used to say, jokingly but with a measure of truth, that all were recruits from the ranks of rugby football. Players past their prime. Portly and secure, but never happy. Beset by conscience, or conscienceless.

After a curt introduction the two men thrust their way into the lounge. Ordering my wife not to interfere, the spokesman for the two said, 'One toot from you and your husband will be put onto the next plane out of The Republic.' (Always it is The Republic, never South Africa or even Suid Afrika, or any loosely descriptive term. The making of The Republic was an Afrikaner achievement, with Godly sanction. Alone they had moulded themselves into a nation, concocted a language, but God's hand guided the formation of The Republic. It is in keeping with the concept of apartheid that there shall be no sharing. It cannot be our land, our country, one people. And while there are other republics, this is *The* Republic).

A routine search was made throughout the house, though from the start the two men knew where their main interest lay, and having found it they spent most of their time in the one room, my study. Letters were scrutinized. Close attention was paid to my reference books, invaluable to me but of no particular interest to men of their kind. I hope they noticed that most were concerned with Africa, though not with separate development. There were no hard core political books, fortunately, and few novels. There were newspaper cuttings galore, representing all shades of opinion. A few days earlier and they could have pounced upon a copy of Edgar Snow's *Red Star Over China*, which had been loaned to me and returned – just in time. I did have a copy of Father Trevor Huddleston's *Naught for Your Comfort*, not on the banned list though not recommended as essential reading. My two personal cuttings files revealed nothing new; most of my political writings had been published locally, and presumably there were copies filed at Security Branch headquarters. My multitudinous jottings and quotations were sifted; what a thankless task that must have been.

It so happened that there was no banned literature in my possession at that time. There might have been, and indeed it had been touch and go. Providentially I had made a bonfire of some old treasures shortly before this unannounced visitation. All were of the most virulent kind of banned publications. There were copies of *The Guardian* (banned 1952), *Advance* (banned 1954), *New Age* (successor to *Advance*, banned 1960) and *Spark* (successor to *New Age*, not legally banned, but compelled to cease publication because of personal banning orders placed upon members of the editorial staff). Also there were subversive pamplets with photographs of the Rivonia Trial accused together with potted histories. I had been most reluctant to destroy these symbols of resistance, but into the flames they went after one reprieve – and not too soon, or I would have paid the penalty for harbouring pieces of paper, and it was not worth the price. Rather the spirit of resistance ingrained in the heart, engraved in the memory. So, after the abortive attempt, the offending literature was fed to the consuming flames.

It is doubtful if the two men expected to find anything really incriminating. They must have been briefed beforehand, and presumably they knew my life story in detail. My wife and I were well known for our community interests, while my views on various topics, including politics, were a recurring feature in the local press.

After the flames had done their work there was nothing to fear. My wife was not a political person, while I was hard hitting in a non-violent sense. The time was not yet right for underground warfare or the violence of the streets. Yet, if asked, the Special Branch men would have found reason enough for their search. It was their duty to apprehend; every vestige of opposition must be quashed at the outset. They had to be vigilant, ruthless, unswervingly loyal to their masters. They must not relent. The struggle, once entered upon, is utterly demanding.

It may be claimed that while house searches are humiliating, they are no more than trifling vexations, and one way in which to avoid them is to be law abiding. Yes, and intimidated.

That the two men went away empty handed from their search of our Redhouse home was fortuitous; sooner or later, in every closet there is found a skeleton, as so nearly happened in my case.

Regardless of the outcome, they had achieved their main purpose. In fact they did not stand to lose. As my wife told me afterwards, they went as they had come, unsmiling. In spite of everything, they had reason to feel pride in duty well done. The message would be passed on to me; 'One toot, and you will be put onto the first plane out of The Republic.'

Personal Reflections
(3)

There were other incidents designed to intimidate and instill fear. My mail was tampered with. Some of the more imposing envelopes of foolscap size, especially those bearing foreign stamps or special endorsements, were opened and afterwards re-sealed with noticeable lack of care. Some were marked 'Official: Opened.' This happened too often for it to be accidental. Worse still, there were indications that other letters had been opened and later resecured without the official notification.

The sense of being under suspicion, of being watched, shadowed, of having one's mail read, imparts a prickly, nettle-rash feeling that does not wear off easily.

'I am not aware of any political offences for which people go to prison in this country.' (Mr B. J. Vorster, Minister of Justice)

'Note well, I am limiting the period to 90 days.' (Minister of Justice Mr Vorster, at introduction of Section 17 (90-Day Clause) of General Law Amendment Act, 1963)

'The object of the insertion of this Section of the Act was not to punish persons; it was not to isolate them; it was not to prevent them from conspiring with other people. It was to obtain information from them . . . That was the official and only reason . . . A detainee need not remain in jail for a single day.' (Minister of Justice Mr Vorster)

'Robben Island is not a jail in the ordinary sense of the word.' (Mr B. J. Vorster, House of Assembly 15th June 1965)

'We go in for a humane line in the prisons.' (Commissioner of Prisons, Major-General Johannes Steyn)

'If Mr Vorster really wants the world to believe that the hundreds of men and women who have been sentenced to prison terms for belonging to, say, the banned ANC are not suffering only for their political convictions, but are real criminals, then he will have to be more convincing in his replies to questions.' (*Eastern Province Herald* leader, 24th Feb. 1965)

'We all know, of course, that this undertaking, made to induce Parliament to accept these wide powers, was not honoured. Of a total of nearly 700 detainees more than 60 have been detained for more than 90 days, and eight for more than 180 days.' (Mr Hamilton Russell M.P.)

'We know that many detainees are kept in their cells for weeks and even months before being interrogated or given a chance to secure their release by answering questions.' (Mr Hamilton Russell)

'I am free to go where I like provided it is not beyond the fence.' (Robert Mangaleso Sobukwe)

'I do not think there is a police station in the country that doesn't use violence during questioning.'

(Police officer under oath, Bultfontein trial, 13th March 1964)

'I wish to state clearly once again that in South Africa no person has been sentenced to death, imprisoned or otherwise restricted because he had protested against apartheid, did not support it or had campaigned against it.' (Mr B. J. Vorster, Minister of Justice)

'In Holland 3,000 people are in jail every day and 2,000 in Belgium. 70,000 people are sitting in jail today in South Africa.' (Mr Japie Basson M.P., Oct. 1975)

'There is more personal freedom in our country than practically any other country in the world.' (Mr B. J. Vorster)

'In no other country, including Russia and Cuba, does the Government interfere more with the private lives of its inhabitants than in South Africa.' (Mr J. Basson M.P.)

'I have a great admiration for Mr Vorster and his achievements. He is a strong man but he must be even stronger.' (Mr J. J. Fouche, Minister of Defence)

'The Minister of Justice today is more powerful than the Prime Minister. He is mostly a law unto himself. The public utterances of Mr Vorster make it clear that he revels in his authoritarian role.' (*Eastern Province Herald* leader, 12th March 1964)

'The only book allowed in the cells is the Bible, and many – especially Africans – do not want it.' 'They have only a Bible to read . . .' (Extracts from two newspaper reports)

'It becomes quite nauseating when one knows that the inventors of this system of barbarity declare themselves to be dedicated to the preservation of Western Christian civilisation.' (Mr Hamilton Russell)

'The natives of South Africa can thank God every day that they can go to the white man with their plates and their mugs to seek food.' (Dominee S. J. van der Walt of the Gereformeerde Kerk)

Out of hearing of his guards, he (Nelson Mandela) complains bitterly of his treatment. He points to his crumpled khaki shorts – 'All part of the cruel method of destroying our dignity.' (*Sunday Times*, London, 25th April 1965)

'As far as its circumstances, institutions and results are concerned, South Africa's prison service compares favourably with the best in the world.' (Dr Verwoerd at passing out parade of probationary warders, Kroonstad, Oct. 1965)

'Notify the prison authorities and you will receive medical attention as good as anywhere else in the country.' (Magistrate to Eddie Ntutu, who complained of injuries received when arrested on charges under the Suppression of Communism Act)

'Death due to asphyxia by hanging. Suicide while in unsound mind. Death was not brought about by the negligence of any person. No blame attaches.' (Findings of magistrate at inquiry into death of Sipo James Tyitya)

'It is a desperate act of a desperate man and the action of a coward.' (Mr J. H. Liebenberg, senior State advocate at Fischer Trial)

'It seems inconceivable, but it is true, that this law (90-Day Clause) makes mental torture an officially acknowledged and ministerially approved instrument of police interrogation.' (Mr Hamilton Russell)

Mrs Norma Kitson, a former detainee, described the weekly visit of a magistrate as 'a screaming joke.' 'Even if he is nice he has no power to do anything but report to the Chief Magistrate. There was never any report back about the state of my husband, children, the house or any legal matter.'

Sipo James Tyitya, a 37-year-old awaiting trial political prisoner, was found in his cell hanging from a window. A green scarf was knotted around his neck and tied to one of the vertical bars. (News report 30th May 1964)

'I can no longer serve justice in the way I have attempted to do during the past thirty years. I can do it only in the way I have now chosen.' (Abram Fischer, in letter written at time of going into hiding, 25th Jan. 1965)

'One may ask Mr Vorster, "What did you do during the last war when you thought your way of life was threatened?" We know that Mr Vorster became a general in an organisation dedicated to overthrow the Government and make South Africa ready for a German victory. He did not apparently trust the ballot box to right his imagined wrongs.'
(Mr Hamilton Russell)

'What did Dr Verwoerd do in those days? He did all he
could from his editorial chair on *Die Transvaler* to
bring down the Government. He went so far as to incur
an adverse judgement of the court that he knowingly
aided the Nazi cause.'
(Mr Hamilton Russell)

THE SCALES ARE WEIGHTED AGAINST JUSTICE

Look not for justice;
    nature knows nothing of it.
Only in the courts of man
    does jurisprudence sit.

Men speak of justice fondly
    and tend it, never tiring
    of their invention,
    until the vain offspring,
    fondling of necessity,
    defeats their best intention.

The seven deadly sins multiply,
    become seventy times seven,
    while the statutes increase,
    and the law makers,
    and in turn the lawbreakers.
Until in desperation
    vexed spirits cry to heaven
    'Preserve us Lord, preserve us.'

Better a degree of virtue
    and a little contrition
    than any amount of justice
                    seen to be done.

Look not for justice;
    nature knows nothing of it.
Only in the courts of man
    does jurisprudence sit.

What price freedom? How to evaluate it?

I count myself fortunate in experiencing an episode in two parts which impressed upon me the wisdom of granting freedom with good grace before it is too late. India was the scene of both occurrences. The first took place in 1946, before the granting of freedom. The atmosphere was tense, so much so that it could be known intuitively. There was no open hostility to me as a visitor, but neither was there any friendliness. The prevailing attitude was exemplified in an occurrence which expressed the mood of the times and was typically Indian in being non-violent.

The scene was Bombay on an oppressive afternoon, with heat and humidity combining to drive me into the shadows. I walked along a pavement with tall blocks of flats to my right. Suddenly there was a distinct 'Splat!' at my feet. Glancing down, I saw a blob of spittle, red with betelnut juice. Looking up quickly, I was in time to see a man crouch behind a balcony on the 4th floor. Obviously an Indian, he must have spat at me from above, not carelessly, by accident, but deliberately. A near miss.

That it was intentional was proved as I continued along the same pavement, comforted by the thought that lightning does not strike in the same spot twice. I passed into the shade of another block of flats. There followed a repeat performance. The sudden 'Splat!' Another near miss. I glanced up quickly as before and saw a shadowy form dart behind a sheltering pillar. Another dark face crowned with pitch black hair, another aggrieved Indian. Not to be menaced a third time, with the odds in favour of a direct hit, I moved off the pavement into the roadway. Despite the traffic, it was safer there.

Wherever I went it was the same, in Bombay and later in Calcutta. As a white man, member of an imperial race, I was not wanted in India. As a symbol of colonialist rule, I was not welcome in a land struggling for freedom from colonialism. The cry was for *swarag*; 'White man, go home.'

A year later I travelled the same route. By that time India had been granted independence, begrudgingly but not too late. The aftermath of sectional riots, Mahatma Gandhi's death and consequent martyrdom, these were events of the recent past. The birth pangs were ending, India was settling into an era of a new and adventurous kind, as a world power in her own right.

The change was astounding. Now I could walk where I wished, in shade or sun as suited me best. The welcome mats were out in Bombay and Calcutta. There was no fear of being spat upon from apartments in high rise buildings. Instead there was kindness and helpfulness wherever I went, whatever my need. Supplanting sullen looks and insolence, there was courtesy and a desire to please. It was the same all the way to Darjeeling and back.

On the first occasion I represented a dominant white race, a colonial power. Consequently I was detested, along with the colonial structure. Only a year elapsed, but in that time there was a change of attitude both remarkable and pleasurable. I was accepted graciously as another, though contrasting, human being, an equal not a peer, fellow member of a commonwealth of nations, representative of a world power willing to withdraw while there was sufficient goodwill remaining, before hatred became ineradicable. The wind of change had been heeded timeously and made to blow for the good of all.

To India my respects. To India my heartfelt appreciation.

My story gains significance when it is recalled that India took the lead in the overall struggle for liberation, establishing a pattern for others to follow, from Ghana to Tanzania, from Algeria southward.

While my personal experiences are sufficient to convince me of the correct course for South Africa, hard core apartheidists are not soon to be swayed. It is most unlikely that anything will shift them short of armed struggle. The danger then arises of a local war spreading to become a world conflagration. That is, unless the opposite should occur, and a third world conflict is taken advantage of to obtain freedom for the oppressed majority.

Otherwise, two alternatives exist. On the one hand there is Dr Verwoerd's exhortation; 'Be like granite, not to yield.' Conversely there is the advice given by Sir Thomas Munro, Governor of Madras in the 1820s, to directors of the East India Company:

'Your rule is alien and it can never be
popular. You have much to bring your
subjects, but you cannot look for more
than passive gratitude. You are not
here to turn India into England or
Scotland. Work through, not in spite of,
native systems and native ways, with a
prejudice in their favour rather than
against them; and when in the fullness
of time your subjects can frame and
maintain a worthy government for themselves,
get out and take the glory of the achievement
and the sense of having done your duty as
the chief reward for your exertions.'

What fine words, what inspiring sentiment. Unfortunately, in the specific case of South Africa, the ruling Afrikaner minority counters all such suggestions with the argument, 'This is our land. We were here first.' Hence the inevitability of armed struggle, which is likely to prove The Fiercest Fight of all in a long and bloody series of encounters, with this one intensified as a result of its connotations of race and colour.

A TIME FOR HATING

Background:

* The Minister of Justice, Mr B. J. Vorster, replying to Mr T. G. Hughes (Transkeian Territories) said, 'Of the 676 offenders who were sentenced to death in the five years from 1960 to 1964, 494 were executed. The highest number of death sentences during the period occurred in 1963, when 170 offenders were sentenced to death, of whom 120 were executed. Last year 129 people were sentenced to death, of whom 85 were executed.' (House of Assembly, June 1965)

* 'South Africa has the biggest daily jail population in the world. 67,000 compared with 3,000 in Holland.' (Mr Japie Basson, House of Assembly, Nov. 1964)

* Mr B. J. Vorster, replying to Mrs H. Suzman, said that 16,887 persons had been sentenced to whipping during the twelve months ended June 30, 1964, and that a total of 79,038 strokes had been imposed upon them. (House of Assembly, 11th March 1965)

* 'Under the dreadful conditions of detention, when I came very close to suicide, my hatred of the policies of the South African Government, and of the men who do the work of the Government, was strengthened. There I saw at close quarters the inhumanity, brutality, dishonesty and the fear of these men.' (Miss Sylvia Neame, one of accused at the Fischer trial, Regional Court, Johannesburg, 1st March 1965)

* An African who wanted authority to make bags, baths, baskets and pillows in Kabah Location, Uitenhage, had his application turned down by the Town Council. The Council's Bantu Affairs Committee recommended that his application be refused. And so he has been deprived of this opportunity of making a living. The Committee in its report quoted a circular sent our earlier this year by the Department of Bantu Administration. The circular prohibits further businesses in African townships which do not confine themselves to the provision of 'daily essential domestic necessities.' (News report 27th Sept. 1963)

* African men and women were endorsed out of the Johannesburg municipal area at a rate of more than five a day last year.
The Minister of Bantu Administration and Development, Mr
De Wet Nel, said that 19,650 African men and women had been
endorsed out of Johannesburg in 1963. 3,103 Africans had been
endorsed out of the Cape Town municipal area and 660 Africans out of the Cape Divisional Council area. (News report 28th
Jan. 1964)

* The whole of Nigel and Dunnottar have been proclaimed
White areas in terms of the Group Areas Act. (News report 19th
Nov. 1964)

* 'The African Christian finds it difficult convincing the non-
Christian that the Christian religion claimed by the Afrikaner
rulers is not a cloak under which they may masquerade as they
entrench themselves in power and dispossess subject races of
their rights.' (Mr George Magqwashe, writing in *Pro Veritas*,
journal of Christian Institute for Southern Africa)

* 'The whole policy of removals, of uprooting hundreds of
thousands of people, is a disgrace to a so-called civilised
country. . . . The word "resettlement" is a total misnomer.
What the policy really means, in the vast majority of cases, is
the destruction of family life, of the community as a whole, and
of the opportunity to earn a living.' (Mrs Helen Suzman M.P.
writing in *Sunday Times*, 3rd Oct. 1982)

* Thirteen Africans were dragged from the dock to the cells
below the Regional Court, Paarl, after being jailed for three
years each for being members of Poqo. After sentence was
passed, the Africans refused to leave the dock and argued with
the magistrate. The interpreter said the men refused to accept
the sentence as they did not know why they were found guilty.
(News report 22nd June 1963)

* Charlie Dyidi, a 57-year-old Transkei-born African and his
wife, Elizabeth, who have lived in Paarl for 15 years, were sentenced to a total of R30 (or 60 days) for being in Paarl for more
than 72 hours without a permit. (News report 22nd April 1964)

* 'Oh God, I loathe apartheid and all it means. This tragedy
here I place at the door of that system.' (Adrian Leftwich, for-

mer president, National Union of S.A. Students, after testifying against his former colleagues, Spike de Keller and Eddie Daniels, at their trial in Cape Town, Nov. 1964)

* The Government will expropriate 1,000 morgen of land belonging to 2,000 Bapedi tribesmen in the Middelburg district of the Eastern Transvaal. The people are to be moved – against their will – to farms in Sekhukuniland. The tribe own the title deeds to the land.

The tribe will be moved because it 'constitutes a Black spot in a White area', according to the Government.

The land will be expropriated, a spokesman for the Department of Bantu Affairs said, 'Because the Bantu rejected the idea of removal in principle.' The Government has offered R342,106 in compensation for land, loss and inconvenience to the people. The Regent, Chieftainess Miriam Ramaube and her counsellors, with the full backing of her people have turned the offer down and have refused to move under any circumstances. (News report 29th May 1964)

* Miriam Ramaube, Regent of the Bapedi tribe of Doornkop, was found guilty and sentenced to thirty days imprisonment by Mr W. J. Pienaar in the Magistrate's court, Middelburg, for having failed to produce books and registers of the ownership of the farm Klein Doornkop. She has been ordered by the court to produce the books to the Commissioner, Mr H. P. Smit, specially appointed to investigate the ownership and occupation of the farm.

'You have chosen to make a martyr of yourself', said the Magistrate. (News report 12th June 1964)

* Several wives of New Brighton and Kwazakele men convicted under South Africa's political laws are being evicted from their homes and endorsed out of the Port Elizabeth area. 'It is a terrible life of suspense, fear and frustration. God help us', said one "political widow". (News report 13th Feb. 1965)

* 'Cruel discriminatory laws multiply each year. Bitterness and hatred of the Government are growing daily. No outlet for this hatred is permitted because political rights have been removed.' (Abram Fischer)

* 'Once we used to shoot as many people as we liked in South Africa, many more than at Sharpeville, and the world took no notice, but now . . . In 1921 there were 163 killed and 129 wounded at Bulhoek and the world took no notice. But today we kill a miserable 70 at Sharpeville and all hell breaks loose; the Security Council meets, the United States issues warnings and newspapers of the world spread it all over the front pages. I can't understand why the world should take so much notice.' (Minister of Justice, Mr Erasmus, in House of Assembly, 25th May 1961)

* 'There is already too much hate in this country. I am afraid that if the world keeps silent when the Government is madly proceeding with more brutality and is trying to take the lives of our most beloved leaders – and boys in their teens – you cannot stop the hatred from overflowing.' (Miriam Makeba)

* The Minister of Justice, Mr B. J. Vorster, said at a cultural function in Bethlehem that the 'vicious onslaught of hate propaganda' against South Africa would be intensified in the months to come. (News report 9th Oct. 1965)

* 'It's an uneasy, shaky peace that is obtained through repression, through police detentions, bannings, tear-gas bombs, bullets and birdshot. Only the naive and the shortsighted would take comfort from such a peace.' (Mr Obed Kunene, editor *Ilanga*, 1976)

* 'Black Consciousness ideology will pass from poetry and rhetoric to violence and destruction.' (John Dugard, Witwatersrand University law professor, Oct. 1977)

* 'The whites wonder what's come over the blacks. They wonder: Why the escalating violence in the townships, the street demonstrations and the "stay away" calls? It's simple: the blacks have come to the end of their patience.' (Mr Obed Kunene, 1976)

* 'Blacks and whites are drifting farther and farther apart and one wonders if ever the twain shall meet. One wonders even about the wisdom of offering solutions in a land where white supremacy is next to godliness.' (Obed Kunene, 1976)

* 'If I were black, I would hate all whites.' (Senator Flip de Jager, Emmarentia, May 1980)

* On September 13th, 400,000 Venda-speaking South Africans were deprived of their South African citizenship and made foreigners and sojourners in their own land. (News report 1979)

* Eric Abraham, a young South African journalist, is currently being subjected to the kind of malicious treatment that the South African government has made peculiarly its own. Banned for five years, Abraham is forbidden to work, to enter a newspaper office or university building, and is not allowed to leave his home from night till morning. In the circumstances, since he is deprived of his livelihood, he has applied to leave the country. But the authorities refuse to grant an exit visa. He is thus trapped, and viciously trapped, by a government that allows him neither to live nor to leave. Worse still, he is subjected to unbridled harassment, death threats and menacing phone calls – that the authorities appear to have no interest in curbing. Nor is this an isolated case. At least a dozen journalists are now in detention held without charge or trial. Their only crime is to have reported and investigated the country's internal troubles in the wake of the Soweto riots. They have been sentenced to oblivion for being good journalists. The South African government may well feel that its own survival depends on the crushing of free opinion. Such measures are a mark of its own desperation. But even by the strange logic of white supremacy, the treatment of Abraham appears vengeful and rooted in malice. (*The Guardian Weekly*, 19th Dec. 1979)

* The Medical Association of South Africa has exonerated the physicians who treated Steve Biko shortly before his death in police detention but will not disclose why it reached this decision. Instead a spokesman for the Cape Midlands branch, Dr J. J. Geere, accuses newspapers of 'stirring up trouble.' (News report 1981)

* In 1982 a total of 206,022 people were arrested for contravening the Influx Control measures. . . . Already about eight million black South Africans have lost their citizenship and been made, arbitrarily, citizens of either Transkei, BophuthaTswana, Venda or Ciskei, all of which have been granted their

'independence.' . . . Police and government officials arrested one black person every 2½ minutes of the year for being 'illegally' in the so-called white part of the country. (News reports June 1983)

* 'We have become the world's best busybodies; the world's most fanatical bureaucrats; the world's arch meddlers, most active and expert trouble-makers. Where there was clarity, we bring confusion; where order, chaos. Where there was quiet harmony, the marriage of true minds, the communion of kindred spirits, we bring discord, jarring disunion, clash and conflict, frustration, suspicion, distrust, animosity, resentment and what is worse than all these – hate. For our hates are growing. And where hate grows, everything perishes away, everything withers.' (Uys Krige, Afrikaner poet, 1965)

'A time to love, and a time to hate';
Eccle. 3:8

A TIME TO HATE

God in Africa
   has strewn so many laws
   of loathing in our way
   it is hard to go on loving
   from day to day.
He must have intended our fall from grace
   for now it is too late, too late
   for anything but hate, hate, hate.

Down-to-earth people of firm conviction,
   worldly-wise and generous, bold enough to care,
   rooted in their resolve, beyond contradiction,
   honest-to-goodness folk everywhere,
   must surely detest apartheid,
   a word tailor-made
   for hurt, for hate.

155

Roll it off the tongue,
  a-p-a-r-t-h-e-i-d,
  it presupposes wrong,
  hints at division,
  invites collision.
Imposed as a way of life
  it cuts with the savagery of a saw-toothed knife.
It mangles, mars and mutilates,
  lays waste to love, and not the least
  bares in human breasts the beast
  it convokes and motivates.
See it for what it is, nothing less
  than a thief of time, a common cheat,
  rough-hewn, lacking finesse,
  a diplomatic shadow-show, a deceit,
  a form of class distinction, of 'us' opposed to 'them',
  fear-inspired, stoked by avarice, ill meant,
  a portentious caste system
  devoid of religious content.

Aspiring to growth, the scholar becomes a teacher,
  gains and gives a wealth, a worth
  of knowledge. So too with nature.
Carefully tended and watered the earth
  yields it crop, passes on its seed. Thus,
  past and future reside in the present, in us.
Giving as we receive, so we prosper.
Weeds of past neglect hinder but should not deter.
Seeking good, in a world of give and take,
  now is the time to eradicate
  Bush Colleges
    Tribal Academics
      University Segregation
        the whole cap and gown
          of education leading down
            to imposed inferiority.

If it is love we look for, and prize,
  and serve to propagate,
  firstly we must fertilize
  a down-to-earth hate.

Abhorrent are the tares of untruth,
   the lie of Separate Development.
Erosive of the soul, the Bantustans
   are patchworks of deception,
   reservoirs of white privilege;
   leftovers from the white man's table,
   handouts of a Hollander,
   creator of a modern fable.

Corrosive of the mind, Homeland Citizenship
   is more than a wilful slip
   of the tongue. When all is said and done
   it remains a fraudulent foistering
                        of false identities
   from Europe without love,
   the white man's folly
   the black man's burden.
To abduct rights makes room for hate;
   Influx Control invokes trespass,
   makes of black Africans sojourners
   in black Africa.

Orderly Movement and Settlement
                     of Black Persons' Bill . . .
   what a mouthful – enough to fill
   a pelican's bellyful.
Stranger, stranger! Resettlement
   creates the stranger
   in our midst, encroaching danger,
   leaving no chance for negotiation,
   no opening for conciliation.
Now must be the time for hating.

Music works magically,
   modulating, marshalling separate notes,
   bringing them together
   as rhythm if not harmony.
Less pleasing, the discord
   of Discrimination,
   an ugly word, a note of dissension
   deserving of hatred.

157

Demolition workers are as worthy
  as builders, and are paid as much.
Both are essential
  to an overgrown civilisation.
As demolishers we should destroy
  the South Africa Foundation,
  gaunt edifice, base, pillar, ploy
  of White Privilege.
Working overtime, yet we shall be late
  in toppling Group Areas,
  the housing estate
  of legislative hate.

For aspiring youth, limited education,
  for willing workers, Job Reservation,
  from first to last, motivations for hate,
  incessantly, until all too late
  for love to flourish.
We cannot compute the loss we suffer
  through negligence, depriving ourselves
  as we deprive others. Call it fate.
Because of failure to relate
  life levies its toll of hate.

As close companions to the Bantustans
  stand Border Industries,
  perched precariously on lone peripheries,
  monuments to arrogance, to avarice,
  symbols of a half-truth, of delay,
  luring hungry workers
  an easy distance away.

But no conspiracy of late
  inspires more return of hate
  than the infamous Pass Laws.
It is as though hidebound lawmakers
  are over-employed, busily manufacturing
                              lawbreakers,

conspiring to formulate
an all-enveloping hate,
a sad, vicious cycle of production
leading to self-destruction.

What recompense can there be
   for freedom lost and lowered dignity,
   what chance for suppliant eyes
   raised to vacant skies?

Waiting. A lifelong vigil.
Waiting for a welcome whisper
   of good replacing ill;
   'I tell you a tithe for your comfort,
   Yea, something for your desire. . . .'
One slender hope to take the place of "naught."
Waiting for the overlong night to end,
   night that is thrice night over us
   and heaven an iron cope.
Waiting for godsend,
   for a change from overwintering
   in a sunny, sunny land.

Reservations of doubt intrude.
Wait for God and you wait for eternity.
Better forget. God has no part in this.
The builder, having built, goes his way.
Forget the creator. While you kneel
   the watchful win the day.
Forget prayer and grab power.
Forget God, get guns.

Resurrections of doubt,
   lapses into despondency,
   change and change about.
Thoughts of tribal ancestors, tribal gods,
   desecrated graves, homelands ravaged,
   rites and ceremonies savaged,
   the past restored while the present nods.

Observing miracles daily, moonwalks,
    machines that skim the waters, barely touching,
                            astounding
    planetary probes, technology abounding
    while we walk here as aliens
    in our own land, wretched earthlings.
As compensation for land grab
    a rented plot, a home handy to hospital,
    situated near cemetery.
Ball games, highly competitive,
    to make men forget
    warfaring on a modest scale.
Commuter trains tearing to town and back,
    the belching chimney stack;
    here, yet fearing to die, we live.

Awaiting relief
    from burdensome grief,
    waiting for release
    from bondage without cease.
Awaiting an end to Resettlement
    in impoverished homelands,
    overcrowded wastelands
    in which to bury one's head,
    impossible dreamlands
    fit only for the dead.
Waiting while the world holds back from the brink,
    thinking the end may be near,
    restrained not by compassion
    but fear.
Waiting, with world watch abated
    by common consent, each nation sated
    with vested self-interest,
    the slow rot, the ruination of the west.

God, behind whose back
    has Africa come to this!
A checkerboard, with squares of White and Black
    kept apart, a Verwoerdian dream, rather a nightmare,
    an ideological battleground

criss-crossed as for trench warfare,
with corpses strewn around,
no victor, only the victim,
no victory, only the grim
gaunt spectre of defeat
and the curses lingering with the dead
and those left to salvage, all too late,
the future with its residue of hate.

The African giant, slumbrous, stirs uneasily.
By nature not vindictive, slow to hate,
    he awakens to black consciousness.
Roused, if not too late
    he must lose his lethargy,
    once his shield from sun and slavery,
    lately his debilitating malady.
Now he needs must activate
    a consciousness of hate;
    so long oppressed, if he is to create
    he must first destroy.

Now is a time to hate:
    not people, but their avaricious acts,
    not people, but their cunning artifacts,
    not people, but their brazen monuments,
                    their graven images.
Not Verwoerd, but his sinister artifice.
Not Vorster, but his craven effrontery.
Not Botha, but his lacklustre policy.

Black man, you are on your own!
Gregarious as before
    but essentially alone,
    in common with the poor.
Those who would help if they could,
                    cannot.
Those who could help if they would,
                    will not.

161

So long neglected,
    what use your rejected
    overtures of love and friendliness?
In the past, so much abused,
    why smile affably, as though amused
    at what the future holds of less and less?
Political pariahs, stripped of leadership,
    your past unfolds
    revealing loss upon loss:
            Nelson Mandela
            Robert Sobukwe
            Albert Luthuli
            Oliver Tambo
            Walter Sisulu
            Steven Biko . . .
Social lepers, outcasts
    in all that matters most,
    you have been outmatched
    in that which matters least.
Denied political leaders, your host
    fobs you off with sporting heroes
    and in place of the common vote
    substitutes a soporific,
    non-racial rugby, cricket,
    boxing, athletics, football,
    one and all
    inclined, as intended,
    to make the leaderless forget
    their jailed leaders, the landless forget
    the peasants' revolt and present plight.
In the name of sport, what ails?
Is it sporting to play fast and loose
    with memories of internees, crowded jails,
    torture cells, the hangman's noose?
Winnie Mandela, her's the bravery at Brandfort,
    your's the sideline slavery.
Winnie Mandela, prestigious, plucky,
    her's the gamesmanship,
    your's the idolatry.
Wars are not won on playing fields.

Not one sport has brought release
    nor one iota of relief
    for a single prisoner. Sport yields
    no measure of freedom.
Trotting onto fields of play,
    trotting off at end of day,
    whites and blacks, each to go
    a separate way.
Thoughtless to treat your leaders so.

Sport? For what good reason?
Sport? Or is it treason?
Sport? Or what passes
        as another opium of the masses?

Now is a time to hate:
    not sport, but predilection
            amounting to addiction,
    not sport, but its diversionary use
            amounting to affliction,
    not sport, but its political abuse,
    not sport as a pastime, but its endless misuse.

Jesus wept. Africa mourns.
Love rests. Fear reigns.
For all its ills, all its pains,
    Africa grows, awaits new dawns,
    and meanwhile finds, albeit late,
    a time to hate.

Comment

There is nothing tongue-in-cheek about my advocacy of un-mitigated hate. If the blacks of South Africa are to achieve full stature in the land of their birth they must shrug off complacency and achieve a significant measure of hate. Other-wise there is no means of retrieving a situation of such utter hopelessness and helplessness. Following in the wake of Black Consciousness, a Consciousness of Hate.

Nor do I mean a lukewarm feeling but a full-blooded, seething, rip-roaring hatred, a thoroughly cleansing hate, aimed not at people but at their institutions founded upon selfishness and greed, with implications of servility, humiliation and degredation, as with apartheid. To meet the need of a people so long oppressed, it must be a marching, militant, magnificent hate. For The Fiercest Fight, which has already started, it has to be deeply felt, a zealous, righteous hate.

Good natured as a rule, naturally smiling and carefree, indolent as a result of abject slavery and continuing near-slavery, isolated from the mainstream of events, the blacks of South Africa have taken long to emerge this far and now need to go that step farther, against almost insuperable odds. Minority rule is mightily entrenched, and supported by one of the great powers, the U.S., so hate must be enlisted to force its removal while every ploy, every shop window dressing manoeuvre is employed to stave off the day of retribution.

Apartheid embodies so many hate objects that the major ones are listed below without comment as a means of clarification:

Separate Development, Race Discrimination, White
    Privilege
Pass Laws
University Segregation, Bush Colleges, Tribal Academics
Job Reservation
Group Areas
Influx Control
The South Africa Foundation
Bantustans, "Homeland" Citizenship, Border Industries,
    Resettlement (Orderly Movement and Settlement of Black
    Persons)
And, as I have pointed out, Integration of Sport as a diver-
    sionary tactic aimed at keeping the black masses amused
    while more and ever more are Resettled in already over-
    populated Bantustans.

THE NEW CRUSADE

Background:

* 'The pincipal and most urgent task of the democratic forces in this country is to remove the Nationalist Party from power and thus rid the country of the greatest single menace to racial harmony.' (Chief Albert Luthuli)

* 'Freedom for the black man in Africa remains the great unfinished business of mankind.' (Mr L. P. Weaver, high negro official in U.S. Government)

* 'On this basic issue the whole world has to take sides and we in Tanzania believe that Africa has the right to demand support for its stand against South Africa. We are not disputing with another country about the organisation of society; this dispute is about the humanity of man.' (Julius Nyerere)

* 'It is not only white domination the Nationalist Government wants, but Afrikaner domination. Their criterion is that this is their country because they were here first. They are not prepared to consider the contribution of other groups, even though the English-speaking people have contributed more to the building of South Africa than the Afrikaner. The point is that this country is the home of the Africans as well, and they do not intend to leave it either. Somehow we have got to live here together.' (Prof. Z. K. Matthews, former vice-principal, Fort Hare University)

* 'The white man is tortured by fear of the black man; fear that some day the African may take revenge; fear that if he opened the gates of freedom he might be swamped. He has made no secret of this fear. Yet instead of making the necessary adjustments to eliminate its causes, he chooses to remain with it, and merely to postpone the day of reckoning by barricading himself. The Christian mind ought to be free from fear and anxiety. It is the guilty conscience that is weighted down with fear. The white man must learn that if you brutalise a man, you must expect his soul to become twisted.' (J. C. M. Mbata, Field Officer, S.A. Institute of Race Relations)

* 'The ignorant demand knowledge, the dependent demand independence. Above all, the underprivileged demand the privileges of human dignity and significance. They want to feel their lives have some meaning, that they have some significant work to do, and that they are given some share in building their nation. These demands are irresistible. They will grow and will somehow be satisfied. White South Africans should not regard the situation as a menace to be met defensively with fear or even with restrictive measures, but as a challenge to be met with faith and positive effort.' (Julian Huxley)

* 'What South African whites require is an imaginative leap forward of the greatest emotional and intellectual effort. In my opinion, South Africans will be forced to unlearn in a few years the results of three centuries of historical conditioning and practices.' (Ruvi Bennun)

* 'It is those who grasp the basic assertion of the Africanism movement who are stimulated by its possibilities, and those who can only see its secondary effects – anti-colonialism or anti-Westernism – who are depressed by it.' (Canon J. S. Kingsnorth)

* 'The time has come to free three million white people from paralysing fear.' (Govan Mbeki)

* 'I did it because I want to free my black brothers.' (17-year-old youth when sentenced to five years imprisonment for writing to a friend urging him to go to Botswana for military training)

* According to the head of security police, Brigadier C. F. Zietsman, 2,500 'potential terrorists' have been brought to trial under security legislation since June 1976. 'You can see it is no longer child's play. It is an extended onslaught we are fighting.' (News report Aug. 1979)

* 'The battle for liberty is not easy. But that liberty we want is worth all these sacrifices.' (Central Committee, FRELIMO, 1967)

* 'Developments in Viet Nam, Angola and Mozambique have shown that a system that cannot be changed peacefully must be changed by arms.' (Oliver Tambo)

* 'We are really moving towards a racial climax, the inevitable racial climax. You can feel the atmosphere, walking in the streets, that we are heading for that clash.' (Winnie Mandela)

* 'I have not only joined you as a daughter calling for the release of her father. I've joined as part of my generation who have never known what normal life is, but know what it is to be without a father and sometimes a mother, not because one's parents have committed any crime, but because my generation have seen grave crimes committed against the people. We grew up discussing the latest pass raids, whose father had been detained, who had lost a parent in detention, or in which prison one of your parents is, when last they were visited, when the last police raid was on your house. . . . This was our childhood conversation.' (Zinzie Mandela at 'Free Mandela' rally, March 1980)

* 'The tragedy is that the black-white war in South Africa has already passed the point of avoidability, and although the whites don't know this the blacks know it well.' (Donald Woods, former editor East London *Daily Dispatch* 1981)

* 'The kernel of the whole issue, which is constantly being played down by the South African propagandists, is that black and white South Africans have already entered the initial phase of a state of war.' (Donald Woods)

* 'Viet Nam is a demonstration that total victory is possible against the greatest power on earth. There is no need for the compromise – really a capitulation – that the moderates offer.' (*The Guardian Weekly*)

* 'In history there are two kinds of wars: just wars and unjust wars. Just wars are wars against oppressors and conquerors to safeguard the freedom and independence of the people. Unjust wars are aimed at the seizure of territory, at usurpation of the freedom and happiness of the majority of the people of such territories.' (Truong Chinh, Viet Nam)

* 'Cetewayo would be embarrassed to see some of us doing nothing about our oppression and exploitation.' (Student leader, Soweto, 1981)

* A New Zealand priest based in South Africa says full-scale civil war there is justified and a certainty. Canon John Osmers said in Wellington yesterday the time for words had long since gone. Now was the time for action. It was possible for a good Christian to be involved in a war for a good cause, he said. 'Internal civil strife will escalate. A civil war? I don't want to put a date for civil war.' (News report 5th June 1981)

* 'As a result of the Government's inability to reform and keep its word, violence and revolution are staring South Africa in the face.' (Opposition MP Mr Horace van Rensburg, August 1981)

THE NEW CRUSADE

Ours' is a modern crusade,
    we march against apartheid.

But
    before committing ourselves irrevocably,
    if we are wise
    we shall pause
    long enough to scrutinize
    all aspects of our cause.
We should heed history's verdict anon
    and in terms of thirty, sixty, ninety years on.
For we shall be campaigning
    in an age of reasoning.

Sincerity of purpose is not enough.
Apartheidists also are sincere. Sincere
    but wrong.
We must be made of sterner stuff.
We must know Right from Wrong,
    take our stand by Truth and Honesty.
From these we gain our strength,
    for they add up to constancy;
    they do not change,
    nor should we.

The culmination of our love
    is in war. We fight because we must.
God knows, our cause is just.

*   *   *   *

Adventurers, Discoverers,
    we are both.
As adventurers we march
    to make sense of sacrifice,
    restore the lost years, lost dignity
    of Chief Albert Luthuli, Robert Sobukwe,
    Nelson and Winnie Mandela, Walter Sisulu . . .
    heroes by now legion, becoming legendary.
We march to make the exiles' wanderings
    more tolerable in retrospect.
We pave the way to martyrdom;
    emblazoned as on shields, in hearts and minds
    these hallowed names now grown
    familiar – Mapetla Mohapi, Steven Biko and some
    equally illustrious but unsung
    because unknown.

When we return it will not be
    to cheering crowds and glory.
There will be no flags flying,
    no feasting, no peace parades.
In one and all the past soon fades
    and judgement day arrives. Our campaign
    will be weighed, found wanting;
    "Why, why so long a reign
    for blatant evil aptly named
    apartheid?"
Out-of-context criticism
    comes easily to the churlish,
    provides for the uninvolved
    an out-of-season relish.

169

Other adventurers have gone bush,
  gone walkabout,
  climbed Everest, K2,
  Nanda Devi, Manaslu,
  travelled transglobe,
  made space probe . . .
  to whose relief,
  for whose release,
  to what end?

As discoverers breaking through
  hostile barriers of fear
  we explore the human race
  and hope to find,
  across lost frontiers of the mind,
  faithful, fearless intentions
  giving to freedom new dimensions
  and to mankind
  a nobler face.

Other discoverers have traced
  the Nile to its source,
  followed Semliki River's winding course,
  pioneered routes, reached the poles,
  crawled into caverns, potholes,
  salvaged seabed treasure,
  pieced together archaean fragments.
All in the name of discovery
  and incidental pleasure.

We sift through distortions of history
  to retrieve the reputations
  of dethroned giants
  of the past, said to have been tyrants,
  Mzilikaze, Dingaan, Moshesh . . .
We seek lost fortunes, the wealth
  left out of history books
  in whose blank pages we now inscribe
  these names of the truly great;

Nkadimeng, Mosenyi, Moredi . . .
peasants all, penniless, poor
though they leave a legacy
enriching us, enough to restore
our own lost treasure
of humility
in fair measure.

*   *   *   *

A few more considerations,
   then to have done with speculation:

GRATITUDE.

            We shall not find,
               and should not expect,
               gratitude. Let there be no pretence.
               If there should be reward
               it will flow from allegiance
               to our Lord.

FEELING.

            Can we take upon ourselves
               the feelings of others
               and make them our own?
               The hurt pride,
               the heaped insults,
               the broadly smiling front that masks
               deepseated desperation,
               the exasperations
               of the damned?

SACRIFICE.

            Are we ready to make sacrifice?
               Of life, if need be,
               that others might live in peace
               unfettered, abundantly?

PAIN.

> We are born to pain.
>   It is not
>   a jestor's joke or demon's plot.
>   Without it, no pleasure, no gain.
>   But can we accept
>   more than our share,
>   more than the common lot?

RACE.

>   Can we take stock
>   of earthbound roots
>   from which we spring willy-nilly
>   and neither envy
>   nor mock?

COLOUR.

>   Can we see it, see through
>   and shelve it, observe
>   and not be blinded, perceive
>   and not permit it to deceive?

RESTITUTION.

>   Trespassing wherever one treads,
>   the greatest, the meanest of thefts
>   the theft of land.
>   Are we ready to return it
>   to its Owner's hand?

COMPROMISE.

>   Who would not prefer
>   to gain results through peaceful parley
>   rather than disaster?
>   Yet the time is long since gone
>   for compromise.

FREEDOM.

>   What of freedom,
>   fact or fantasy?
>   What price freedom?

172

Is it worth the sacrifice
or is the cost too high
this dice
with death?

DEFEAT.

Can we face defeat
and declare it temporary,
await the turn of tide and see
beyond to victory?

FEAR.

What motivates the enemy?
The Devil incarnate.
What compels? Fear, the handmaid
of the Devil drives.
Our duty is clear:
to rid our land of apartheid,
to exorcise fear.

DEATH.

Can we look on life, on death
and declare the one irrelevant
while bringing to the other a breath
of heroism?

*　　*　　*　　*

Having explored within, without,
beyond the last shadow of doubt,
then to be zealous.
Not for us the vacillating turnabout,
the compliant deviation;
leave that to Leftwich and Paton.

The Tempter
        speaks:
                "In all things good
                        there is some evil,
                        in all things evil,
                        some good."

Thus are our forces sundered, spent,
        split by doubt, torn by argument.
We must not permit the heartbreak
        of indecision. War is never good
        but it can be just.
Apartheid is never good
        and cannot be just.

                When one is said to be the other
                        and neither good nor bad,
                        where is the border drawn
                        and how is doubt resolved?
                War with suffering,
                        peace under apartheid,
                        which the lesser of two evils?

War brings death or glory,
        apartheid, unrelieved suffering and humiliation,
        an altogether different story.
Doubt and indecision
        go hand in hand.
The swift incision
        of our action, our crusade,
        will hurt the enemy
        no more than the oppressed
        are hurt by apartheid.
Ideally, compassion is for friend
        and foe alike.

It was wrong to presume
        an end to slavery.
Because surveillance waned too soon
        there came whiplash restored,

as though to signify that victory
is incomplete without vigilance.
Apartheid and slavery
are one and the same,
an age-old addiction, a new name,
the naked clothed
and deemed respectable.
This is the heart of the matter,
giving rise
to all that follows.
In our crusade
we oppose slavery
in its modern guise.

Now, having done with reasoning,
let us put on the full armour of faith,
hereafter to be clear of vision,
never again plagued by indecision.
For we are crusaders, believers,
history makers, retrievers
of lost dignity, restorers
of stolen pride.
This the good fight,
the new crusade,
we march against apartheid.

Personal Reflections

When the early white settlers arrived in southern Africa they showed commendable skill in unravelling the mysteries of language and custom. They took note of unusual rites and ceremonies, particularly those associated with sex. Occasionally they were baffled, as by the absence of places of worship. Mistakenly they concluded that religion was lacking. They paid no heed to the close affinity with nature, at its best a form of worship as sincere as any organised religion. Especially mystifying was the absence of boundary markings. Wishful thinking led them to believe that the land belonged to no one. In that case, it may as well belong to them.

Really the land did not belong to anyone in particular, but to each and all. There was no such restrictive measure as trespass in the open veld until the whites, claiming ownership, split the land into lots, whereupon there was trespass and the need for laws relating to trespass. In following train there came into being a form of greed called land hunger, a human failing hitherto unknown in these parts.

It was presumptuous for the newcomers to suppose that the land was theirs for the taking, it was wrong for them to conclude that the indigenous tribes held no religious beliefs. What they failed to take into account were the invisible attachments. It is a fate worse than death to be robbed of one's identity, deprived of one's ancestry, torn from one's history, forced from the friendly tradition of sharing in a community spirit as old as the tribes, forced to forsake the fireside council (democracy at its best) and made to accept an alien materialism with its accompanying commercialism of cash. Most degrading of all is to be counted a trespasser in one's country of origin.

The land grab! This is the crux of the situation. In South Africa the struggle is for the land. To whom does it belong? Whose the prior claim?

With few exceptions, school history books state authoritatively 'The Dutch were first at the Cape.'

Conversely it has been declared (I quote) 'I don't have much faith in history books that try to put across the story that a group of whites were the first settlers in the southern parts of black Africa.'

Certainly Van Riebeeck made no claim to priority. Later comers did that, masking their theft of land with a cloak of righteousness.

The Khoi-Khoin, or Hottentots, were at the sea's edge as Jan van Riebeeck and his men waded ashore. They were helpful, not hostile, because earlier callers at the Cape had left them in peace. That there had been others before them is known, as also the fact that Autshumao, the Khoi-Khoin chief, had acquired a useful knowledge of English. So Van Riebeeck was not the first white seafarer to land there. Nor was he the first settler. Naturally these historical facts do not serve the National Party cause or lend support to the patriotic cry of *'Ons land'*. So government propagandists and biased historians have combined to reshape events. No wonder that history is said to be bunk. In many instances it is. In this case the 'big lie' operates as it did in nazi Germany. Tell a lie often enough and it will be accepted as truth. Through distortions of history, one generation inculcates in others the belief that white privilege is a birthright, that security of tenure is vested in visions of a chosen people.

What are the known facts?

In 1658, a mere six years after his arrival, Van Riebeeck noted in his Journal: 'With 20 to 30 good soldiers, 15,000 to 16,000 sheep or oxen might be taken without a blow.' Already flocks of sheep and herds of oxen were in vast quantities. From where had they come, that so many might be stolen?

Who was the initial transgressor? At an early stage there were accusations as to which side started thieving from the other. From the written testimony of Van Riebeeck there can be no doubt. Two years later he received a delegation of Hottentots 'who dwelt long upon our taking every day for our own use more of the land which had belonged to them for all ages.'

This statement provides adequate proof as to who were the first settlers at the Cape, whites or blacks. In mitigation of the white settlers' behaviour it has been said that the times were hard. So they must have been for the Hottentots also. Yet they were pastoral people, well disposed, not warlike. Of the two parties they were the better behaved. They may not have washed as often as the whites, but they did not stoop to the deadliest of sins, greed, taken to its ultimate in the theft of land.

Van Riebeeck's entry continues: 'They also asked, if they were to come to Holland, would they be permitted to act in a similar manner?' So, not only were there black people at the Cape, but they were mannerly enough to question the morality of the invaders. But they were not strong enough, or rude enough, to drive them from their territory.

As soon as their first few trinkets had been bartered away, the newcomers established a pattern that was to serve them well if not honourably. They started by stealing sheep and cattle. Then, the livestock needing land on which to graze, they stole the land, taking more and ever more for their own use. At length the dispossessed blacks, with nothing left to lose, were pressed into service as slaves. When slavery was partial, payment was minimal and even that was considered too much, so that "hut tax" was devised. The idea was that more should be required in back payment than was given out in wages, thereby ensuring permanent indebtedness, lasting slavery. When the form of slavery was absolute, that was that, without prevarication.

As for Bushmen, also on the spot in those early days, they provided excellent sport. In fact they were hunted like baboons. It is recorded that, in 1774, a Boer commando killed 503 for the loss of one white huntsman. Between 1785 and 1795, a single decade, no fewer than 2,504 were killed by hunting parties, according to official figures. What I find especially interesting in these sordid statements is that all those years ago, long before the modern tragedy of Viet Nam, a body count was made. Also the kill rate is noteworthy. Standing at 500 to 1 and more than 2,500 to nil, it was not approached in Viet Nam despite absolute mastery in the air and unlimited use of napalm. The times were ruthless, yes, but need they have been that ruthless?

Now let us consider the Strandlopers. Relics have been unearthed in caves along the Tzitzikama Coast, proving the existence of these coastal folk hundreds of years before the arrival of Van Riebeeck. It would be understandable if Afrikaner claims to the land were based upon right of conquest, but this is not the case. The insistence upon exclusive right is rooted in "first come, first served".

This being a scientific age, there is need to provide scientific proof in support of one claimant or the other. It exists, and the facts do not support the Afrikaner view. Ironically, it was an Afrikaner archaeologist, L. Fouche, who revealed the evidence when excavating a Sotho site in Northern Transvaal. His findings proved the existence of Sotho tribesmen within seven miles of where Johannesburg stands today. Modern dating methods prove their occupation of this site in AD 1200 or earlier. In 1970 an engineer, while roadmaking in the Transvaal, came upon pottery, beads and metal objects which were carbon dated AD 270–300. Later archaeological evidence supports the conclusion that Bantu-speaking races were in southern Africa 1200 years before the arrival of European settlers. It is well authenticated that the main body of Xhosa tribesmen was established as far south as the Fish River when the first white settlers arrived. That is, they occupied territory in line with the present site of Cape Town. Smaller bands were in the vicinity of the Tzitzikama Forest. These people were nomadic, moving from place to place to prevent their livestock from overgrazing the land.

No wonder Afrikaner history books and Government handouts are vague in relation to dates of arrival: 'Blacks and whites arrived about the same time' or 'Blacks and whites arrived more or less simultaneously.' To quote Dr Verwoerd, the architect of separate development, 'We settled a country bare.' It was the self-righteous Afrikaner speaking, clearing the land, making it appear conveniently bare. It is different when seeking to extoll Voortrekker valour. The land must not be shown to be empty, devoid of opposition. For a display of heroics there must be redoubtable opponents and plenty of them. To fit the need, 'everywhere there were marauding hordes of Kaffirs.'

When it pleases the Afrikaner to show how truly he belongs, he points to his tribal name, African-er. When reserving public seats and open spaces for his exclusive use, he is just as pleased to reveal his European ancestry by marking these places '*Alles vir Europeans*' – For Europeans Only.

It must be one way or the other. We cannot alter rules of play to suit our purpose of the moment.

Afrikaners cannot be Africans because they are not black, and all along they have stressed the difference in colour between Europeans and Africans. It is they who drew the distinction of colour, they who wove a pattern of legislation based upon colour. Already it is too late to turn and say that colour is of no consequence. Suddenly it is, to the extent that it denotes the true landowner and the usurper. Presented in terms of black and white, the truth is that no whites have originated in Africa. The original inhabitants of the African continent were black, coal black, pitch black, black black. Black Africans do not hold their origins in doubt. They do not assume European ties. They do not have to put on an act. Their roots are in Africa and they abide by the truth, which lends them strength.

The words of an American soldier returned from Viet Nam hold relevance. Expressing his disillusionment he said; 'There was just no way to beat the political fact that we were foreign and they were out of the soil.' So it must prove in South Africa now that the fight is on. The Afrikaner strives to show that he is not foreign, but in denying the rights of others he falsifies his own right to be in Africa as a ruling minority. He alienates himself as he seeks to alienate others. His effrontery has given rise to the Black Consciousness movement. Thus are the strident brought down and the meek uplifted.

No wonder the youngsters of Soweto and other ghettos wish to clear away old deadwood and reveal the truth, which surfaces when banalities are swept aside, when subtleties are expelled.

In earlier days of exploitation, millions of blacks were taken from Africa forcibly. We have a word for it. We say they were Uprooted. We apply this word because of the widespread belief that we spring from the soil and to the soil return. It is the source of all that is born, the homestead of all that lives, the graveyard of all that dies. The earth nourishes us, and in return we must care for it. Take away from the soil without affording it replenishment and we steal from ourselves. Defile the earth and we defile ourselves. To rob others of their birthright is personally unrewarding. We gain by giving, not by taking.

As a minority, ruling autocratically, the Afrikaners cannot be sure of the time left to them as overlords. They are not unaware of the Big Lie, nor of the fact that truth must prevail sooner or later. They must know themselves as foreigners, descendants of settlers whose power and possessions sprang from the barrels of their guns. Deep within, it must be realised that the land which they refuse to share was not gained the way their historians and propagandists claim. Bluntly, the early settlers perpetrated the greatest of all crimes, the theft of land. It follows that those who have taken over from them are receivers of stolen goods.

This reminds me of a case of land theft which took place toward the end of my time in the Eastern Province of South Africa. It involved a choice piece of Tribal Trust Land beside the Tzitzikama Coast, granted 'in perpetuity' by Queen Victoria. It was annexed as quietly as possible in order to avoid voluble protest. Once the blacks had been removed, the whites moved in. With smooth efficiency the land was taken over, passing from Africans to Afrikaners. One more black loss, one more white gain. One more wrong to be redressed.

There is a passage in Hindu scripture to the effect that, through lack of the principle of relationship which binds us as one, men and governments appear to prosper, gain all they desire, triumph over their enemies – but perish at the root.

From this it can be inferred that Afrikaner racist rule is endangered, not from without but from within. So far the National Party appears to have prospered, having remained in office longer than any other government of today. It has succeeded in smashing all attempts at organised resistance to its apartheid policy. It has triumphed over the Liberal Party, the ANC, the P-AC, *Umkhonto we Sizwe*, the S.A. Students Organisation, the Black Peoples Convention, Black Consciousness and all others. Armed victories have been won at Sharpeville and Soweto, to mention but two, with body counts vastly in excess of the 10 to 1 ratio which satisfied American militarists in Viet Nam. Thanks to Verwoerd's brilliantly conceived, devisive Bantustans, Africans are being forced back to tribalism against their will, also to economic dependency. Every African who might have aspired to leadership has been killed, imprisoned, banned, banished or driven into exile. Afrikaners have triumphed over their rivals to the last one. But at what price?

A situation has developed in which white supremacists have become victims of their own contrivances in support of the Land Grab. These range from brute *baaskap* to the deceit of apartheid and the ultimate treachery of "homeland republics" and "resettlement". To gain all they desire, Afrikaners have had to employ every mean political ploy, including the infamous High Court of Parliament. Stopping at nothing, they introduced torture and faked suicides into their prison system. But not without cost to themselves. The fall has yet to come but the rot has set in, as shown by the scandals of 1979 involving some of Afrikanerdom's brightest if not best, including Dr Connie Mulder, Dr Eschel Rhoodie, Gen. Van den Bergh and former Prime Minister Mr B. J. Vorster. Thus, while appearing to prosper, Afrikanerdom is in the process of perishing at the root.

The land grab. This is the eye of the storm. This is what the struggle is about. If the unarmed peasants of Witzieshoek, Marico, Zeerust, Pondoland, Sekhukuniland had not revolted, nothing could have saved the indigenous races from perpetual apartheid rule. And if the exiles, in growing number, had not remained true to their cause, nothing could have been organised from outside to relieve the pressures within. Once again it is seen that help, when it arrives, must stem from the two sources, not from one alone. Although Afrikanerdom is in the process of disintegration, the rising generation of blacks cannot await its slow attrition. Direct action must be taken, no matter what the price in suffering and death. Attempts to redress wrong must be made, or it becomes a case of condoning evil by allowing it to prosper.

In case there should be any lingering hope that detente may provide a way out, it is worth considering a fairly recent pronouncement by the National Education Minister, Mr Piet Koornhof. In what was described as a cautiously worded speech, the minister said that South Africa's need could be met with 'cultural pluralism, meaning equal co-existence in a mutually supportive relationship within one nation of people of different colours, cultures, languages and beliefs.' This complex statement reminds me of a cartoon showing a white lift attendant explaining to a black man, 'Apartheid, separate development, vertical differentiation – it all means *you can't go in.*'

When words become meaningless the gun takes over. In the light of such pettifogging verbiage it is clear that only through cleansing revolution can there be anything approaching a solution, one that deals with basic principles, stemming from the soil, ending with the land.

Now is the time for black Africans to take up the cry 'We want our land back.' Nothing less will suffice. The cry has been raised before, but prematurely. Now is the time for its renewal.

No one should be misled by the earlier call of 'One man, one vote.' It had to be made, and in those terms. Now it is different. In the political climate of today it is possible to be entirely frank about the struggle as it has developed. No longer is it a clamour for mere voting rights. It is a struggle for the land. This is a part of the African continent: who owns it?

Really it should not matter so much as to who arrived first, blacks or whites. If, from the start, the attitude had been one of fairness in sharing, all may have been well. If the whites had adopted the same belief as the blacks, that the land is God-given and not negotiable, as though it were pieces of silver, there would not be the need which exists at present, of calling upon hate and reaching for the gun as a means of arbitrating between the races as to who shall govern.

In confirmation of this attitude there are the words of Nelson Mandela upon returning from oversea to the land of his birth, there to be imprisoned for the rest of his life: 'People say I made this war. Let me see whether my delivering myself up to the conquerors will restore peace to my country.'

It did not.

In its own terms, invoking struggle, ensuring sacrifice, the truth rings out:

> When progressive change is checked in its course,
> when there is a thwarting of evolution,
> the only alternative is revolution.

IN CONCLUSION
(1)

It was not my wish to end on a drear note of desperation, to point to hatred as a need and war as a culmination, the like of which has not been known before. No, but neither is it my intention to distort history and detract from its likely consequences in order to raise false hopes. Rather a mature, calculated pessimism than an impractical optimism based upon wishful thinking.

Were I to seek vindication for my harsh realism and uncomfortable conclusions, it comes from an isolated but by no means singular incident to which I have drawn attention briefly (Personal Reflections, The New Crusade). It concerns the forced removal or "resettlement" of Fingos from fertile farmlands alongside the famed Garden Route between Humansdorp and Nature's Valley, in the Eastern Province of South Africa. Supposedly held in trust (and if Governments are not to be trusted, who is?) the farmlands are situated amid beautiful scenery with a climate of near perfection, fringed to the south by the awe-inspiring and ruggedly lovely Tzitzikama Coast, and to the north by a chain of mountains. For the Fingos this must have represented the good life, with security of tenure.

But, as with Job Reservation, covetous eyes were turned in their direction. The pounce, the Land Grab, was due to take place.

Came the fateful era, in the late 1950s and continuing through the 1960s, with Verwoerd and apartheid, Group Areas, the Bantustans and forced migration . . . and an end to security. Granted in trust by Queen Victoria, the coveted land was disposed of by Dr Verwoerd and his followers. Mounting repression, then the ouster followed by years in the wilderness counting the cost, feeling the loss, years of unavailing pleas, of attempts to redress a gross injustice. Although an outsider, and white, I felt the fury of repression as though I were directly involved.

After a lapse of 25 years, a quarter of a century, the following news report, of recent date, came to my notice:

> A delegation of Fingos is expected to listen to a
> Parliamentary debate on how they lost their land

184

held in trust for them for 140 years. A special debate
is planned to consider a report of a Parliamentary
Select Committee which investigated irregularities
revolving around excision of the land in the
Tzitzikama area and subsequent Government offer
of its sale to white farmers.
The select committee found nothing irregular in the
Government handling of the land deal but
Opposition members on the committee supported a
declaration that the entire manoeuvre was irregular
and a breach of trust.

An accompanying report gave vent to human considerations. It
confirmed my deepest suspicions, upheld my contention that to
let bygones be bygones in a case of such immensity is nothing
short of cowardly.

This second report told how a 'desperate band of Fingos' left
Port Elizabeth for Cape Town in an eleventh-hour bid to plead
with Government to allow its people to go 'home.' A spokes-
men, Mr Izak Tembani, said the Fingos' final stand followed
repeated attempts to draw Government attention to their cause,
though little hope of a reprieve was held out.

'If nothing else we will just be there in the visitors' gallery of
Parliament to witness how our land is taken away from us' said
another delegate, Mr Robert Maqungo.

Mr Tembani said he hoped to plead with the minister directly
concerned, Dr Koornhof, to return their rightful land. He
described the conditions under which they live in "resettlement" at Elukhanyweni as appalling, with little food and
money, and no work.

'The land at Tzitzikama was fertile. In the new place the land
is arid and nothing will grow.' He described his people as con-
fused and bitter. Also they were resentful when told by Dr
Koornhof that they should consult what he called 'your own
government, the Government of Ciskei' about the matter.

Another delegate, Mrs Msizi, said they had complied and
had been told to 'speak to Pretoria, we don't have anything to
do with you.' In short, driven from pillar to post, frustrated at
every turn.

As though this were not enough, the Fingos face intimidation from the authorities in Pretoria who say they should no longer refer to themselves as Fingos and speak about their 'home' near Humansdorp (an Afrikaner stronghold). 'They say we must forget we are Fingos and become Ciskeians.'

Mr Tembani said the delegation, for which more than R600 was raised through donations and fund raising activities, would meet members of the Opposition in Cape Town to seek advice. 'If they tell us there is nothing more we can do, we won't give up, we'll just consider what we can do next.'

What to do, what to do? Where next to turn in a world wherein the scales are weighted on a racial basis. They look in vain who look for justice. Neither can there be any emotional appeal. Only hypocrisy and deceit can thrive where apartheid flourishes.

These reports prove beyond a shadow of doubt that, while *klein* apartheid is being relaxed here and there, especially in sport where it is most noticeable and available as propaganda, *groot* apartheid is being intensified. While self-seeking MPs, so-called sportsmen and other dignatories from abroad turn a blind eye, forced migration, falsely termed resettlement, continues with mounting fury, bringing enduring hardship, ingrained bitterness to the dispossessed. While visiting players clamour to indulge their peculiar whims, pretending that they are breaking down racial barriers, the Verwoerdian vision of one vast unbroken domain for whites and separate "homelands" for non-whites becomes a reality.

In South Africa there is a saying frequently quoted by whites in relation to the Bantustan divide-and-rule policy, to the effect that an egg, once scrambled, cannot be unscrambled. Visitors under the auspices of the South Africa Foundation are aware of this; but, to their shame, they leave behind the residue, an irretrievably broken land. It needs no sort of prophet to foretell violent confrontation born of utter frustration.

Here are the facts of the Fingo loss of land and liberty presented without embellishment:

25 years of deprivation.

25 years of the greatest theft of all, the theft of land.

25 years of unutterable misery, of striving to subdue the memory.

25 years of unavailing appeals for decency to prevail.

25 years, a quarter of a century, of wretchedness.

But it is not the poor and dispossessed who are the wretched of this earth so much as those who create wastelands of deprivation in a world of plenty. Sometimes this is done through ignorance, itself inexcusable, more often as a result of avarice.

Taking into account all that I have revealed, especially this narrative of brutality, it will involve self-deception and lies on the part of those who claim that apartheid is on its way out, given time and non-interference. This is far from the truth where 'brute' apartheid is concerned. Indeed, it is well on its way to claiming its victims, even unto the third and fourth generation of the guiltless.

I know the Tzitzikama intimately, and I know the African as well as most. Black Africans are easy-going to their own detriment, forgiving to a fault. They smile so broadly, not because they are pleased but to mask a monstrous desperation. As I have pointed out, they have one option left – to obey the injuction A Time to Hate. I have seen the smiles fade, the clenched fists go up. After Black Consciousness, A Time for Hating.

Epilogue

While the manuscript for *The Fiercest Fight* was being readied for publication, renewed outbreaks of violence took place in South Africa and a State of Emergency was declared. Events of this nature lend substance to all that has been assembled here, and there is little to add, although I have been asked to append a few words. In this there are pitfalls, apart from that of prophesy, for I agree with Obed Kunene who is quoted as saying 'One wonders even about the wisdom of offering solutions in a land where white supremacy is next to godliness' (p. 153).

On the other hand it is essential to note that this is the first war in which one side is massively armed, the other completely unarmed. Therefore history affords no comparison, provides no indication of what the future holds. As Bishop Desmond Tutu said when receiving his Nobel Peace Prize, 'We are going to be free, about that there can be no doubt. We ask only How and When?' I too have wrestled with this seemingly insoluble problem, and have come to this conclusion: if we knew *How* we should lose what little power we possess as individuals to sway the course of events; if we knew *When*, we would cease from striving. Full knowledge of the *How* and *When* would take away the essential element of mystery and leave us bereft of mastery.

Really, the disparity in arms is regrettable, because it lengthens the conflict and leads to a body count akin to that suffered by the Bushmen, as recounted in the chapter *The New Crusade*. Not only this, but it is to blame (along with the tri-cameral parliament which lends a voice to Indians and Coloureds, but not Africans) for the deplorable attacks upon Indians in Natal Province. It becomes a case of 'We can't get at the Afrikaners, so let's have a go at the Indians'.

For the ruling whites there are a few options available. They may be listed as follows:

1. Attempts to wheedle round the Americans, the most likely of foreign powers to salvage Afrikaner dominance.
2. Reformist policy. Tried already, resulting in that colossal blunder, the tri-cameral constitution. (This, and the accord with neighbouring states, left black South Africans in no doubt as to their complete isolation and powerlessness).
3. An approach to moderate black leaders, primarily Chief

Gatsha Buthelezi of KwaZulu, the most likely prospect. This could provide a welcome respite. Meanwhile Nelson Mandela, an ageing man, might die, relieving President Botha of a meeting which he would rather not make.

4. Historically, the most feasible outcome is for the laager mentality to prevail.

5. Unconditional release of Mandela and his colleagues and the calling of a national convention. After 25 years of refusal, this is unlikely, though it offers the best prospects, with consequent relaxation of the detested Pass Laws and Influx Control, thereby permitting non-whites to move freely in search of work and settlement. Inevitably this would mean that the more wealthy of non-whites would be able to reside in areas formerly reserved for whites. Difficulties would arise initially but time, the great healer, could resolve all issues, as also with completely integrated education. Hardened racists would pack and go but others would adapt. The Bantustans would need to be abolished, and to this end Nelson Mandela's leadership could provide the essential key. I feel strongly that if Nelson is not released in time, unconditionally, then black South Africans will be driven to widespread violence spilling into white areas.

As for the numerically superior Africans, they are left with no option. They must come to realise the futility of tackling armoured vehicles with stones. Their only recourse is to assemble a massive hatred, so potent as to make them ungovernable under white racist rule. Let me put it this way:

Apartheid came into being as an *idea* circulating in the mind of one man only, born in Holland – Verwoerd. And because it was an idea whose time had come, it developed a power of its own. In fact, when time and circumstance are favourable, ideas possess immense, almost limitless potential. Therefore, being weaponless, deliberately split into tribal enclaves, black Africans have no alternative but to relocate the burden of fear, swinging it from themselves, the voteless majority, to the whites, the racist minority. To achieve this, they need to reverse the tide of hate, while taking care not to become trapped, as the whites are. They must limit their hatred to the system of oppression which enslaves them, and not vent it in racism and the colour of the skin.

For, not through hatred is hatred appeased. Hatred is appeased through not hatred. (Don't forget, we are dealing with the realm of ideas, in which words are inadequate). Hatred must be seen for what it is, not an evil of itself, but a counter-force against a palpable evil. The urge to destroy in order to create afresh, to purify.

Staying with the world of ideas, we can see the role which non-Africans might play in the eradication of one of the greatest evils of all time. We can join in a campaign of unbridled hatred, directed aright. That is, not against people, not against those who operate an evil system of government to their own advantage, but against the evil itself, so aptly named apartheid.

Born of hatred, apartheid can be eradicated only by means of an opposing force of sufficient intensity. Thus it is said that there is a time to love, a time to hate.

Don't ask me why, but we live in a universe in which it is necessary to destroy in order to create. For there to be life, there must be death. Thus it can be said that, alike to the urge to love, the urge to hate is a creative force. Love and hate are different sides of the same coin, as it were.

In the case of apartheid and the 'resettlement' policy, the need to hate is allied with the desire to create a fairer system of government and thereby give rise to love in place of hate. Rightly directed, our hate will have no ill effect upon us. We need to overcome fear, set aside anger, control hatred. We are dealing with an idea, remember, an idea whose time has come, than which there is nothing stronger.

In truth, a revolutionary situation exists. The ruling Afrikaner National Party created it, and in so doing they inherited a legacy of fear, so that they now fear a counter revolution, because the gun may conquer but it cannot control. And in the face of overwhelming numbers Afrikanerdom is encountering increasing problems of control. For the first time ever, the initiative has gone from their hands.

Paraparaumu   Earl Denman
 New Zealand 1985